YOUTH LONGS TO KNOW

Explorations of the Spirit in Education

YOUTH LONGS TO KNOW

Explorations of the Spirit in Education

JOHN F. GARDNER

& Anthroposophic Press

Copyright 1997 by John F. Gardner

Published by Anthroposophic Press
3390 Route 9, Hudson, NY 12534

Library of Congress Cataloging-in-Publication Data

Gardner, John Fentress.
    Youth longs to know : explorations of the spirit in education /
John F. Gardner.
        p. cm.
    Includes bibliographical references.
    ISBN 0-88010-445-7 (paper)
    1. Teaching—Religious aspects.   2. Education—Philosophy.
3. Anthroposophy.   4. Adolescence.   5. Play.   I. Title.
LB1027.2G37   1997
370'.1—dc21   97–11408
                                                            CIP

10 9 8 7 6 5 4 3 2 1

Printed in the United States of America

CONTENTS

PREFACE

I consider it an undeserved privilege to be asked to write the preface to this book. This is all the more true as I have nothing wise to say in its support. Wisdom is hard to find or come by today, as most realize. The ones who are most aware of this are those whose deepest longings have not completely disappeared under the world's wheels. At twenty-six years old, it was not so long ago that I was a youth myself. Perhaps by some definitions, I still am.

Young people have their problems, it's true, and the middle-aged have theirs, and the old their own. But young people have so much before them, so much still to come—or not—that the overriding, haunting question is one of hope: Is there any hope for the young? Any hope that they will understand what needs to be done to save the world? Any hope that they will find what they love and do it? Any hope that they will find their souls, not lose them?

I don't know whether these questions are new or have always been with humanity's youth. They are real, though, and vastly important. I personally suspect there have never before been so many young people who have not known their place, not known what to do, or how, or why.

Are the youth today—we youth, I should say—looking for someone with answers? Are we seeking advice? To a certain degree, yes. It is nice to find someone who talks common sense, someone who talks real experience, and knows herself or himself without illusion. In fact, nothing else is acceptable.

In a much bigger sense, however, no, we are not looking for advice. The reason is not hard to understand. Even good advice—answers and directions—come from without. They don't answer, finally, the longing from within, the need to be self-directed and self-found. What youth asks for (in this I am surely one) is to be shown itself: itself as ideal. It asks to be shown the true human being, and what follows from this vision. Then one need only follow one's own heart, one's own seeing—and one can *do* this, too.

This collection of essays by John Gardner appears to be informed by such a vision. This vision is not a scheme, and so these varied essays seem to come from quite different places, and draw different pictures. They are for the most part alive, breathing a wisdom that is yet imperfect, but all filled with and aspiring toward the spiritual ideal of humanity.

Thankfully, there is no presumption of knowledge here, or unhelpful advice. The words are words of genuine common sense (the kind Mark Twain said was very uncommon), of deeply felt and pondered experience. The very few spots where this experience thins—such as in the discussion of those exalted stages of knowledge Steiner has shown the world—can be completed by turning to those wonderful souls and sources John himself calls attention to.

This book offers some answers, but they are of the sort that need to be completed by the reader. And this is welcome. I cannot value any book for another person. But I will tell you that this book shines with gentle, joyous hope.

GENE TALBOTT

FOREWORD

Since these essays were written some years ago, the social-spiritual climate has changed considerably, and yet the young person's search remains basically the same. Disappointment in this search can lead to rebellious, self-destructive behavior. But, whereas the young people of a preceding era can perhaps be characterized in general terms, the differences among them that were then barely discernible have now become marked.

Perhaps the outstanding trait among many young rebels today is not that they "long to know," but that they are so certain that they already know, or are at least hot on the trail. Taking information as knowledge—such as the information being offered by computer technology and the global internet—they feel ready to enlighten those laggards who presume to be rearing and teaching them. In just a few years the "communication" era has come into its own with a vengeance!

Differences in the approaches among young people, however, have deepened. Now we seem almost to be dealing with different traces—not of color or creed, but of human destiny. There are those of a decidedly materialistic bent who are well satisfied to be in pursuit of the obvious. They look forward to making a lot of money, gaining power, and enjoying the worldly thrills thus made possible.

A similar yet distinct group finds its thrill in the spellbinding magic of new technology. It gives them what they want to know—intimate information about the miraculous subtleties of mechanisms. They are entranced by this adventure and seem to be heedless of where it will lead.

Perhaps neither of these groups would admit at this point that it "longs to know" in the sense of this book's intent. Both feel that technological wonders will supply what they imagine to be most important in their lives. Technology enables them to increase their knowledge with impeccable precision and logic. They believe they are well on the way to real insight.

On the other hand, there are youths—disappointed by both ordinary and technological prospects—who are losing themselves to the lure of drugs, sex, and violence that accompanies the so-called communications revolution. They are caught in physical deterioration and psychological depression. The suffering that follows their pursuit of pleasure is obvious and sad.

The issue treated here is relevant to all of these types. But it will perhaps be *comprehended* by a much smaller group (let us call them the idealists favored by fortune). They have seen the dangers that threaten their friends and are alarmed by the course taken by so many young people. They reject the whole mood of a culture that finds computer wizardry so beguiling that many now hope it will lead to a renewal in education. In their desire to help, these young idealists are doing their best to discover the cause and cure of what is so aggressively asserting itself in our time.

My discussion focuses upon this last group because it comes nearest to possessing the clear awareness that is missing in the others. A growing hope tells this group that, within human souls, there is a dawning of the necessity as well as the possibility of achieving an objectively true yet subjectively satisfying relationship to the spiritual realities of life. This last group, it seems, also includes parents and teachers who, during the

1960s, passed through this same phase of wanton and random—though idealistic—rebellion. They have now matured enough to at least glimpse the spiritual life they instinctively sought years ago.

This mood of dissatisfaction, irreverence, and disobedience, however, did not begin in the 1960s. Earlier in Europe it was known as youth's unmanageable "storm and stress." For example, in 1921 during a lecture on education by Rudolf Steiner, one listener rose with these words:

> Parents sometimes have the feeling that they no longer have any say in anything, and that one must simply let these young people go their own way. On the other hand, one witnesses the disillusionment of such an attitude, and it is painful to see young people not finding what they were seeking. There is something in the air that simply seems to forbid a respectful attitude toward older people, something ... ever ready to strike against authority in whatever form.... Why are (the young) not happy? It saddens us that we are no longer able to reach them. I have sought help by studying books dealing with this problem, but I have so far not found a single one that could show me the way forward.[1]

Because these essays were written over a considerable period of time, they do not follow closely, one upon the other, either in their content or style. But there is, I trust, a considerable

---

1. Rudolf Steiner, *Waldorf Education and Anthroposophy 1*, Anthroposophic Press, Hudson, NY, 1995, pp. 127–128. Also, in connection with this prefatory note, I strongly recommend the book by Stephen L. Talbott: *The Future Does Not Compute: Transcending the Machines in Our Midst*, O'Reilly and Associates, Inc. Stabastapol, Calif., 1995.

continuity in the grouping. The relationship between what we call *knowledge* and the higher truth that is *wisdom* has been a lifetime preoccupation for me as a student, educator, and father.

Recently my first book, *The Experience of Knowledge,* was more pointedly reissued as *Education in Search of the Spirit.*[2] With the years, my reflections and experience have grown steadily in the direction indicated by this title. Many today are similarly moving toward the same goal. May they find encouragement as well as some new leads in the following pages.

JOHN F. GARDNER

---

2. First published as *The Experience of Knowledge* by Waldorf Press, Garden City, New York, 1975; revised and updated edition, *Education in Search of the Spirit,* Anthroposophic Press, Hudson, NY, 1996.

YOUTH LONGS TO KNOW

Explorations of the Spirit in Education

1.

YOUTH LONGS
TO KNOW

I am very content with knowing,
if only I could know. —R. W. Emerson

THE URGE TO FIND HIGHER TRUTH

Many children today bear within them greater potential than
ever before, powers that the world needs as never before. Educators and parents must recognize and find ways to encourage
these new capacities. However, children receive educations
and are exposed to habits of thought that do not help, and
what longs most to be fulfilled is frustrated. Our civilization
represents a concerted attack upon the potentials of the newest
generation, and they need our help to withstand it. We must
make it possible for young people to realize their purpose in
life, which is to achieve what they instinctively long for. The
modern world needs this now in order to solve its increasingly
enigmatic human and environmental problems.

It is characteristic of young people that what appears first as
longing, later becomes accomplishment. Young artists are
often powerfully drawn to music, color, and form before
gaining the capacity to use them creatively. Some young students are fascinated by the business world long before they are
able to do anything significant in business. For others, certain

figures seem large in history. In their powerful attraction to
such personalities, they are reaching out for their own latent
capacities. For all young people, what stands out at first on
the far horizon is indicative of what they will eventually produce from their own depths.

Animals

What the souls of most modern young people—whose
strange ways often perplex and dismay—are really seeking is a
deepened experience of life, to be gained through forces lying
almost hidden beneath their present consciousness and impa-
tiently demanding attention. Essentially, these forces have cognitive roots, but they are directed toward and nourished by
very different kinds of knowledge than usually recognized and
cultivated by parents and teachers. Thus, the urge for higher
and deeper experiences of truth is very strong in young people,
although this is often obscured by apparent indifference or
antipathy toward rationality in general. The young turn
against conventional forms of knowledge simply because they
have not found in them the higher truths they seek. Even
before we recognize that their search for truth has begun, they
are often intensely disappointed with the empty and false
world that adults have built.

or have found them untrue

When youth's quest for a more vital knowledge is frustrated, it turns into rebellion against parents, schools, society,
and the prevailing standards of morality. Youth wants to
make sense of life; but when it seems senseless, young people
find fault with all the custodians of culture who allegedly
stand for sense but seem to make nonsense out of existence.
In a sensible life marriages would be filled with love, old people and professors would be wise, the leaders of society would
be heroes, and practical people would be managing affairs so
that nature and humanity prosper, peace would triumph, and
beauty and health would advance. These things, however, are

not happening. Lurking in many children today is the conviction that truth is a much higher experience than anything their parents and teachers have in mind. Truth must be approached through other methods, on some different path. Whatever worthwhile goods ordinary scientific knowledge has brought us—and they are many—it is now at the point of diminishing returns. Young people see that we are spoiling our Earth existence faster than we are improving it. They conclude that, if a more competent knowledge is to appear, currently established forms and procedures of knowledge must abdicate; and their first reaction is rebellion.

Unfortunately, the instinctive goals of the young are not necessarily matched by an ability to reach these goals on their own. Youth must still be guided by those who are older; young people are absolutely dependent upon age to show the way. Yet, they must sense that this way leads to new goals and not to a repetition of the old. The time has come when we must discover what youth is about and what it wants. This discovery is possible if we study the youth scene symptomatically—and if we heed the prophetic forerunners of today's youth (that is, the more advanced souls of yesterday). It is especially helpful to bring an open mind to this century's most essential and comprehensive prophet, one who spoke of the spiritualization that leads from the intellect to wisdom of the heart and soul.

The Bread of Life

Many are seeking the same bread of life for which youth hungers. They have smelled its aroma and even tasted it. They have reliable clues concerning its nature and appearance. We will hardly find another modern thinker for whom the gates of wisdom knowledge have so fully opened as they have for

Rudolf Steiner. His extraordinary, practical achievements support his claim that they were based on the development of capacities for higher knowledge that slumber unknown in everyone, and which it is the very purpose of further human evolution to enlighten.[1] The religious writer Emil Bock suggested that the young ardently seek, though unconsciously, the kinds of experience Steiner described in *The Stages of Higher Knowledge* and elsewhere.[2] In his opinion, youth's frustration in this quest provides the best clue to their otherwise enigmatic and dismaying behavior. Dr. Franz Winkler, from a medically oriented perspective, has made the same analysis.[3]

Briefly, our present thesis is that young souls today hunger and thirst for three new powers of soul, all of which are functions of the cognitive experience. They want first of all to experience life *as* life, with vitality and immediacy. And they long to find a meaning in life that transcends the conventional goals and routines. And they long finally to touch the ultimate higher ground of being in themselves, in others, and in nature. They would like to see the whole world in God. The power that can fulfill the first longing was called *Inspiration* by the idealists, romanticists, and transcendentalists of the last

---

1. On Rudolf Steiner's life and accomplishments, see Rom Landau, *God Is My Adventure*, Faber & Faber, London, 1935; A. P. Shepherd, *A Scientist of the Invisible*, Inner Traditions, Rochester, VT, 1987; Rudolf Steiner, *The Course of My Life*, Anthroposophic Press, Hudson, NY, 1986; Gilbert Childs, *Rudolf Steiner: His Life and Work*, Anthroposophic Press, Hudson, NY, 1995; Friedrich Rittelmeyer, *Rudolf Steiner Enters My Life*, Floris Books, Edinburgh, 1982.
2. Emil Bock, *The Apocalypse of St. John*, Floris Books, Edinburgh, 1986; *The Stages of Higher Knowledge*, Anthroposophic Press, Hudson, NY, 1967.
3. *Man: The Bridge Between Two Worlds*, Harper & Row, New York, 1960; "The Mythology in Wagner's 'Ring' Series and in 'Parsifal,'" *Proceedings*, The Myrin Institute, New York, No. 16–21.

century. Rudolf Steiner chose the same term. He called the second power *Inspiration*. The last power, because it penetrates to the core of existence, he said deserves the name *Intuition*.

Let us see whether certain preferences and hungers that seem to motivate modern youth so obscurely and painfully actually reveal nascent capacities for just these higher kinds of knowing, which adults have the responsibility of recognizing and supporting in education. Then we can proceed to see what, under existing circumstances, becomes of such capacities.

Imagination

Children hunger for imagination because they want to experience life. Their unconscious instinct would like to moisten the dry dust of everyday experience and quicken the heavy body of the world being. There is a longing for buoyancy and flowing movement in themselves and in all beings.

Although adults can perceive external bodily movement well enough, we do not ordinarily perceive the hidden movement that is actual life. Our thoughts are mere images that name life and growth without living and growing themselves.

And yet it could be otherwise. It is natural for small children to live with the wind *in* its blowing and with the white clouds *in* their sailing. Very young children are so close to the falling rain, rising vapors, flowing stream, and shining sun that they participate directly in these living movements. They also bring objects imaginatively *into* movement, which for adults remain inanimate.

In adolescence, youth still preserves the taste for living motion, although it is beginning to dwell more in ideas. Nothing could suit adolescents better than that thought itself moves and lives. They hunger for imagination, because imagination is precisely the ability to think in moving, living pictures. No one has stated the case for imagination better than Emerson. For him, it is imagination that first opens the human soul to the real life of the world, because "the nature of things is flowing," and "the quality of imagination is to flow and not to freeze."[4]

> If in any manner we can stimulate this higher form of knowing, new passages are opened for us into nature; the mind flows into and through things hardest and highest, and the metamorphosis is possible.[5]

Thinking, as it learns to follow life's fluent self-transformations, is itself transformed. It becomes pictorial and its pictures move. Thinking becomes seeing.

> Imagination is a very high sort of seeing, which does not come by study, but by the intellect being where and what it sees; by sharing the path or circuit of things through forms.[6]

Imagination is the ability to see knowingly and to know seeingly. It transforms both facts and thoughts into something new, making what is outward more inward so that it can be felt. It makes what is inward more outward so that it can be vividly seen and grasped. Thus, on the one hand, imagination lifts and lightens material existence until it can be experienced by the human heart; on the other hand, it draws down and condenses immaterial thought to where it becomes creative in the practical world.

---

4. Emerson, "The Poet."
5. Ibid.
6. Ibid.

When a concrete fact is truly imagined, it dissolves, as it were, into currents of life. We approach the living reality out of which this fact has been precipitated. When an abstract idea is fully imagined, on the other hand, it fashions for itself a visible form. It becomes a picture whose creative power is felt. Through imagination we see how "mere" ideas could have brought forth, as Plato taught, the physical world in the beginning, and how they continue to introduce new forms of reality into it now through human artistic and moral initiatives. Concerning the advance from abstract thought to the living imagination, Emerson reminds us that "Whilst we converse with truths as thoughts, they exist also as plastic forces."[7]

Anyone who has difficulty with the idea that imaginations are more than pale thoughts freed of logic and experience and allowed to move about whimsically, should consider the following characterization by Steiner:

> The pictures of Imagination have a vitality and comprehensiveness with which the shadowy memory-pictures of the sense-world—even the glittering and ephemeral physical world itself—cannot be compared. This, too, is a mere shadow compared to the realm of Imagination.[8]

All *becoming* is a fluent, buoyant, process. What has already become, however, is by comparison static and heavy. When, through imagination, the sense for becoming lightens the burden of factual experience, and when through imagination the sense of becoming gives weight to otherwise weightless ideas—transforming abstract thought into formative power—the soul

---

7. *The Complete Writings of Ralph Waldo Emerson*, Wm. H. Wise & Co., New York, 1929, p. 1248.
8. *The Stages of Higher Knowledge*, p. 8.

is doubly invigorated. It can live in the present, breathing in and breathing out. Education should establish this breathing process so that children may stand as living souls between the worlds of matter and spirit, and through their breathing bring about this creative interpenetration.

Inspiration

Idealistic youth longs to see with the eyes of the soul, through imagination. It longs also to hear with the soul's ears, and breathe with the soul's lungs. Youth would add to its experience of the world, in creative, living pictures, the further experience of the world as utterance and tone. Rudolf Steiner called this experience *Inspiration*:

> If anything at all in the realm of sense can be compared with this world of Inspiration, it is the world of sound opened up to us by the sense of hearing—not the sounds of earthly music, but purely "spiritual sounds." One begins to "hear" what is occurring at the heart of things. The stone, the plant, and so forth become "spiritual words." The world begins to express its true nature to the soul. It sounds like an exaggeration, but it is literally true—that at this stage of knowledge one "hears spiritually the growing of the grass." The crystal form is perceived as ringing; the opening blossom "speaks" to the human soul. The inspired person is able to proclaim the inner nature of things; everything rises up before the soul as though from the dead, in a new kind of way. A language is spoken that stems from another world, and that alone can make the every-day world comprehensible. [9]

9. Ibid., pp. 8–9.

Music is the soul's air. The soul of youth longs to hear the singing and sounding of the world, to experience natural and human life as a dance. When the world-process becomes melody, harmony, and rhythm, the human beings can step forth in tune and in time with events—indeed, they can introduce their own counterpoint into the dance of atoms, into the song of the elements, into the harmony of the spheres. All this is known to the musical, breathing experience of knowledge called *Inspiration*.

Few of us can conceive of the future experiences of knowledge that many young souls today are already given to discover, and for which we all deeply long. We would be incapable of characterizing inspiration if it were not for poets and artists who foreshadowed what humankind as a whole will reach one day. Dr. Richard Bucke said, for example, "I have heard him speak of hearing the grass grow and the trees coming out in leaf."[10] As a young man Emerson himself wrote:

The world ... should be like the Dance of Plotinus in which "the bodies are moved in a beautiful manner, as parts of the whole," man moved and moving in ecstasy.[11]

He said that every fact and feature of nature taught him what his office should be, as a professor of the Joyous Science, a detector or delineator of occult harmonies and unpublished beauties ... an affirmer of the One Law, yet as one who should affirm it in music and dancing.[12]

---

10. Richard M. Bucke, *Cosmic Consciousness*, Dutton & Co., New York, 1923, p. 216.
11. Emerson, quoted in Van Wyck Brooks, *The Life of Emerson*, E. P. Dutton & Co., New York, 1932, p. 50.
12. Ibid., p. 49.

Bronson Alcott spoke of moral inspiration as the blissful moment when one abandons one's self to the spirit: "The highest duty is musical and sings itself." And Pope Paul VI told a group of musicians that music is "a most valid instrument in the promotion of humanity and indeed spirituality, for it draws us—perhaps unconsciously—closer to that God who is light and peace and fruitful and living harmony." Carlyle's meaning is the same when he asks, "Who is there that, in logical words, can express the effect music has on us?" Music, he says, is "a kind of inarticulate, unfathomable speech, which leads us to the edge of the Infinite, and lets us for moments gaze into that!"[13]

Emerson affirmed that whenever we are finely enough organized, "we can penetrate into that region where the air is music." In "The Poet" he says:

Like the metamorphosis of things into higher organic forms is their change into melodies. Over everything stands its daemon or soul, and, as the form of the thing is reflected by the eye, so the soul of the thing is reflected by a melody. The sea, the mountain-ridge, Niagara, and every flower-bed, pre-exist, or super-exist, in pre-cantations, which sail like odors in the air, and when any man goes by with an ear sufficiently fine, he overhears them and endeavors to write down the notes without diluting or depraving them.[14]

Emerson's experience is echoed by his friend Carlyle:

---

13. Thomas Carlyle, "The Hero as Poet," *On Heroes, Hero-Worship, and the Heroic in History*, Oxford University Press, London, 1957, p. 109.
14. Emerson, "The Poet."

A musical thought is one spoken by a mind that has pene-
trated into the inmost heart of the thing; detected the
inmost mystery of it, namely, the melody that lies in its
soul, whereby it exists, and has a right to be, here in this
world. All inmost things, we may say are melodious; naturally utter themselves in Song.... See deep enough, and
you see musically; the heart of Nature being everywhere
music, if you can only reach it. [15]

Intuition

Even when the world is made alive and life begins to dance,
sound, and speak itself, a third longing in youth desires something still more fundamental; the human being ultimately
wants to know the world as the manifestation of divine *being*.
Beyond the passing life and soul of things, there is a hunger for
intuitions of eternal spirit.

The power to know was called by Emerson a "resistless men-
struum," a fire that dissolves solid facts. The logical analysis
used in ordinary thinking chops the manifest world into blocks
of ice that we call scientific facts and laws. Imagination melts
this ice into flowing life. This water of life is then further dis-
solved by inspired knowing into air—into the all-pervading
musical soul that in the creative order of things is higher and
earlier than mere life. Finally, air becomes fire, inspiration
becomes intuition. Behind the speech of the world, the highest
form of cognition finds the One Who Speaks. A deeply hidden
part of youth knows even this experience to be possible and
longs for it, as do all human beings.

---

15. Carlyle, op. cit., p. 108.

In "The Over-Soul" Emerson said:

> The soul's advances are not made by gradation, such as can be represented by motion in a straight line, but rather by ascension of state, such as can be represented by metamorphosis—from the egg to the worm, from the worm to the fly.[16]

When imagination has risen to become inspired, and inspiration in turn has ascended the further step to become intuitive, the "resistless" fire of knowing comes into its own. Reaching through derivative life and soul to the causative, creative spirit-fire within and behind all beings, cognition at last arrives.

It has been said that "fact is the *end* or *last issue* of spirit."[17] The *present* form of science cannot confirm this pronouncement as evolutionary truth; but the longing of youth is for the kind of science that can. This longing is really the first stirring of the very powers that will be able to achieve such a science based on intuitive experience.

According to Rudolf Steiner, the ordinary individual experiences, or can experience, one true intuition. That is the initial realization of selfhood, or the *I am*. The certainty of this inward experience rests upon the fact that it begins with the beginning. It confirms itself: "I am because I will to be." In this case, what is to be *known* is at the same time what *I* bring into existence; therefore, I know it beyond the shadow of any doubt. I know it from its own point of view, which is mine. There is no room here for obscurity or doubt in this experience of self-identity.

16. Emerson, "The Over-Soul."
17. Emerson, "Nature."

If there is anything weak about my intuition of my own core of being in *I am*, it is only because I have not come to the still moment when I realize that in this, of all events, I am the absolute prime mover. In the intuition of self-existence, cognition and will are entirely one. This archetypal experience shows, therefore, that intuitive knowledge may be characterized as the *cognitive* use of our deepest creative power; it is *will* that has been wholly transformed into *knowing*.

Intuition in this meaning is the highest form of knowledge, for it alone cancels the separation between knower and known. And if it can be applied to other beings as well as to oneself, it finally becomes possible to overcome the split between subject and object, self and world. Steiner speaks of this achievement as follows:

> The attainment of this stage ... is marked by a very definite inner experience. This experience manifests in the feeling that one no longer stands outside recognized things and occurrences, but is oneself within them. *Images* are not the objects but their imprints. Also *inspiration* does not surrender the object itself, but only tells about it.
>
> What now lives in the soul, however, is in reality the object itself. The I has streamed forth over all beings; it has merged with them....
>
> The actual living of things within the soul is *Intuition*. When it is said of Intuition that "through it the human being creeps into all things," this is literally true.... Perception of the I is the prototype of all intuitive cognition. Thus, to enter into all things, one must first step outside oneself.[18]

---

18. *The Stages of Higher Knowledge*, op.cit., pp. 9–10.

Obviously intuitive cognition is the highest form of love, for complete love is the full experience of another as one's self. Intuition is love that has become knowledge, or knowledge that has become love. The first beginnings of intuition are the answer to the loneliness, the alienation, young people feel so painfully today.

Every soul longs for the experience of love. But we parents and teachers have never given our young people the clue to finding love through cognition. We have given them no hint of what is possible when thought becomes pure devotion and devotion becomes pure thought.[19]

Youth under Attack

What is happening today to young people's longing for life, soul, and spirit in the world and in themselves? Such longing is being frustrated, and the new capacities for both cognition and creation behind the longing are either atrophied or transformed into counterforces. The longing to know the world in a more intimate, soul-satisfying way all require that the organizing mind—as well as the feeling heart and creative will—be enlisted in the quest for truth.

Emerson believed that it is only in the depths of human experience that we can find and fathom the depths of world-reality. But, as he also observed, in actual life the marriage between the human soul and the world is not celebrated.[20] It cannot be celebrated by modern youth, because science has not accepted the validity of any such deepening of knowing. Until it does, our worldview will become less and less meaningful,

---

19. "In the uttermost meaning of the words, thought is devout and devotion is thought." Emerson, "Nature."
20. Ibid.

and growing human beings in their loneliness will become even more uncertain, disappointed, and distorted.

There seems to be a psychological law that if positive powers are suppressed at their own level, they become active as negative powers on a lower level. In today's youth we are seeing appropriate (though unfulfilled) longings transformed into destructive drives. The terrible strength of the latter is drawn from the unfulfillment of the former.

Instead of helping Imagination develop so that it can live into the reality of the great world picture, our society is besieging and assaulting young people with images that destroy imagination and make experience of the phenomenal world even more opaque than it is for the ordinary state of mind. The attack of distracting and distorted images comes from many directions— fast cars and planes, television programs and movies, and the barrage of audio-visual "aids" in classrooms. Young people reach avidly for these images because they do not understand what they really want to picture and experience. They embrace what is actually most alienating to their heart's true desire.

The less help one receives in rising to living images, the more one hungers for passively received substitutes. And the more passively one receives images, the more one's imagination atrophies. It would be helpful if the images that assail young people came from noble sources and had creative power; but they do not. Most of this unremitting blizzard arises from materialism, greed, and lust. It seeks to awaken appetites, not capacities. It appeals to the lowest rather than the highest.

The ear, too, is mercilessly assaulted. While the inner ear longs for the soul's speech and music, the outer ear is deafened with a bombardment of noise unheard before. Consider the unnerving screech of subways, the banshee wail of jets, the draining roar of car traffic. Think of washing machines, vacuum cleaners, and blenders, of lawn mowers, chain saws, and jackhammers. Against this background of incessant mechanical noise, impose radios, stereos, televisions, and videos. We may be genuinely grateful for the service, convenience, or entertainment provided by each of these noisemakers, but let us ask ourselves: What is the ultimate effect of such a cacophony on the human soul?

Youth drinks in the rampant mechanical sound and wants still more. Youth goes to sleep with the stereo on and cannot wake up or eat breakfast without a radio. With earphones on their heads, young people walk the street, tuned in to rap and out to the world. They welcome the juke box in restaurants and the steadily mounting volume of sound at the movies.

We can expect a third kind of attack to be even worse, because it will feed on the frustration of the deepest, creative powers in the soul. Young people truly want to *be* and experience the *being* of others. What they get are corrupted cravings for the cruel assault of sexuality, which, in the final analysis, constitutes the ultimate weapon employed against youth's deep desire to *be* and to know *being*.

The invitation in the advertising, the fashions, the novels, plays, music, and dances appeals to many appetites and impulses, but most of all to sex. It evokes not spiritual fire, but bodily craving; and the misconceived fire of this craving can consume spirit, soul, and life alike.

What Becomes of Youth's Potential?

We have spoken of high powers that long to be fulfilled, and of the corrupted expression of these longings at a lower level when they remain unrecognized. We have seen that *when productive spiritual powers are unexercised, they turn into consuming physical appetites*; these appetites constitute the ruthless attack waged by modern civilization against the humanity of today's youth. What becomes of youth's potential as a result?

Every teacher recognizes that the attack by lifeless, mechanical images is destroying vital imagination. Children are losing the power to draw mental images out of written symbols; they read with increasing difficulty and decreasing stamina. As they grow older, children are also tending to look unimaginatively at nature—at beast and flower, at rock and cloud; too often, they are uninterested. All of nature withdraws from them because they cannot follow her forms with living imagination. At the same time the shaping power of thinking itself also suffers; *creative* thinkers continually fight abstraction by *imagining* what they apprehend.

The negative trend goes even farther in modern art. Here, synthesis—the enhancement of reality toward the ideal—is too often replaced by fragmentation, haphazardness, or merely mad impulsiveness that expose the artist as lacking any control. Meaningless pictures, junk sculpture, theater of the absurd all indicate that the deteriorating use of creative imagination is moving toward a suicidal will to destroy creative power itself.

Canned music and mechanical noise in general are producing progressive tone-deafness in the population at large. Music teachers recognize that children's voices are growing huskier, lower, more limited in pitch, and less willing to sing. Tones produced prematurely by young children in the chest and body fail from the beginning, for it is not the body that sings, but the soul that sings in and through the body. In childhood, correct singing begins high and free as an inner activity. It gradually descends into the body as deepened tone as the body matures. Husky tones in children indicate that the soul and spirit has descended too quickly into the physical.

The bombardment by sound has further effects. The voices of public speakers are increasingly amplified and radios and televisions turned up. Dance music has become electrified and deafening. With the volume increased, melody and harmony are lost, as well as the subtleties of rhythm. Popular music has degenerated to raw beat and thud. Such excess in music has become anti-music.

All this has implications that go far beyond speech, music, and dance as they are usually considered. When they decline, so also belief in a meaningful order of the cosmos declines; so does the capacity to manage social life with peace and justice and the ability to live one's individual life expressively with melodic style, harmonious feeling, and rhythmic power.

We come again to what is deepest and most precious. How is the attack of eroticism affecting the creative and intuitive capacities and the spiritual life of youth? It not only robs young people of intuition, creativity, and love, but causes these normally positive forces to take the path of self-destruction. As a result of the exploitation of sex, too many youths are actually becoming anti-intuitive, anti-creative, and anti-loving. Too many youths are already nihilists, and the end is not in sight.

Why should misused sexuality affect intuition? How are they related? When the deep fire of sexuality sacrifices itself for the high love of truth, knowledge is empowered. Through sacrifice the deepest level of *creative* power becomes highly *cognitive*. Such knowing fully deserves to be called *intuition*. But when sexuality is inflamed and squandered in a purely physical, immediate way, intuition is destroyed. Knowing is swallowed by unknowing, darkness replaces light, and spirit is lost in matter. Further, the suicidal process does not stop with a crippling effect, but progresses to complete negativism. One ends up hating both the knowing spirit and the creative spirit. Do we not see this apathy, turbidity, and dark malice spreading in the ranks of unfulfilled youth?

The constant appeals to physical sexuality draw forces downward that would otherwise live at a higher level in the heart and brain. As sex is squandered the heart grows colder and the brain grows more vague. Such a heart and brain cannot rise above materialism. They tend, rather, to create an environment that will be still more disappointing to the soul, making even more soul forces available for conversion into sheer bodily appetite— an appetite that cannot possibly satisfy itself since it is devouring the soul, and only the soul is capable of experiencing real satisfaction. This prospect is terrifying, and modern youth is immediately confronting that prospect. It may breed heroes or monsters, and teachers are beginning to see signs of both.

This is all related to a strange paradox; amid this emphasis on sexuality, normal sexual vitality may be diminishing as a consequence of exploitation. Preoccupation with a subject often indicates an unconscious realization that the substance of the matter is disappearing. This is just as true of sex as it is of the human fellowship in society, about which we talk so much. The substance of *healthy sex* in the human world is *love*. The death of love (which is inevitable if soulful, spiritual cognition is foiled) subverts the forces of mind, feeling, and will that should have established the intuitive relationship between *I* and *Thou*. The strength, the beauty, and the ability to give or receive happiness are thus removed from sex. What is left is impotence, masked by orgiastic fantasy, sadistic violence, and other artifices.

Thus far, we have not mentioned drug abuse. The search for an expanded consciousness is most obvious in this case, and the suicidal effect of frustrated idealism is becoming equally evident. It is clear that the adolescents who experiment with drugs are seeking intensified perception, the appearance of new and dramatic images. They seek escape from the humdrum and entry into the transcendental. The aim is ecstasy—essentially, no doubt, religious ecstasy. Too many young people believe that drugs hold promise of imagination, of inspiration, of intuition.

Drugs do not, however, deliver on their promise. Whereas they work in diverse ways—none of them well understood—they all have one thing in common; exploitation of the powers of thought, feeling, and will that should bring a better future. Drugs waste the future and achieve an illusory fulfillment in the present. They leave their abusers uninhabited. Thrills are bought at the expense of thought, for thinking, which is first eclipsed, ends in apathy; at the expense of feeling, for the feelings that follow in normal life are dull and torpid; at the expense of will, for the surest sign of a drug user is indecision, a lack of initiative, and creative bankruptcy. The *longing* is justified, but the method of satisfying it is false and suicidal.

Strong Rays of Light

The picture is dark but not black. Strong rays of light shine in the darkness; behind the clouds the sun is still there and has the power to break through. Among the bright rays are many young people themselves. Teachers occasionally see evidence of a new kind of youth among us.[21] These young people are

---

21. See Franz E. Winkler, M.D., "Rays of Hope in a Dark World," The Fellowship Committee of the Anthroposophical Society in America, New York, 1966, p. 9.

remarkable in two ways: they really *want* to do well, and, when given a little sound advice at critical moments, they have the strength to succeed. In them, the powers needed for a spirited form of knowledge are poised for a leap forward.

We also see a whole new climate of thought and feeling among the young that is encouraging and widespread. The love of nature is growing in a way that could not have been predicted a few years ago. Readiness for a simpler life is no longer uncommon. External comforts are willingly, even eagerly, forsaken for inwardness, comradeship, and creative activity. The spirit of Saint Francis seems to be abroad in many quarters, though too often it is the aftermath of, or still associated with, practices that exhaust rather than to build. One encounters among the young today remarkable honesty as well as tenderness in human relationships. These traits, coupled with willingness to accept the pain of self-knowledge, indicate in many young people a purpose that will yet force open the gates leading from sickness to health, from death to life.

To support the young people who are striving to achieve the kind of development the future will demand, there are here and there individual adults—authors, statesmen, ministers, doctors, educators and others—who can offer sound counsel, friendly encouragement, and even inspiring example. Above all, there is the legacy of Rudolf Steiner, especially the educational insights based on his wisdom.

It was Steiner's view that our present age begins something new in human history. The whole sequence of recorded history has been a descent of the human spirit into materiality, with a consequent darkening of spiritual forms of knowing. The ever-increasing brightness of physical perception and scientific intelligence has meant deepening darkness for spiritual perception. But now the tide has turned. Steiner agreed with the Eastern wisdom tradition that the necessary millennia of darkness are to be succeeded by an age of Light, inaugurated in our time. According to this insight, we are witnessing the dawn of the new impulse upward, out of materiality, but at the same time an unequal struggle between this new impulse and the massive, not yet halted, downward momentum of that recently ended long age.

The sign of the new day, according to Rudolf Steiner, is that some people are beginning to realize that cognition can and must break out of its straitjacket. In his *Intuitive Thinking as a Spiritual Path: A Philosophy of Freedom,* Steiner restored the basis for confidence in the power of thinking to know Truth.[22] He later described how thinking can retain the clarity and objectivity of scientific method while developing greater strength by enlisting powers of the soul not used for cognition.[23] It is time, he said, to move beyond improving the physical instruments and techniques of scientific observation, and to refrain from the drive to technologically exploit the physical laws discovered. It is time to focus our attention on thinking itself. The inherent force of thoughtful wakefulness, upon which human freedom and all human progress depend, is now declining. This decline must be reversed.

Thinking must be resuscitated through a renewed confidence in it—revitalized by efforts to place our deeper soul powers at its disposal. Under such conditions, the capacity for objective thinking will begin to develop. Thinking will finally be able to cope with the continually higher levels of phenomena that await proper knowledge. When intellectual cognition

---

22. *Intuitive Thinking as a Spiritual Path: A Philosophy of Freedom,* Anthroposophic Press, Hudson, NY, 1995; previous translations were entitled *Philosophy of Spiritual Activity* and *Philosophy of Freedom.*
23. *Goethean Science,* Mercury Press, Spring Valley, NY, 1988.

evolves to the further capacity of objective *Imagination,* it can know living beings for the first time in their aliveness. When it approaches the *soul* on its own ground, it can rise higher to become *Inspiration.* It must ascend higher to *Intuition* in order to know the primordial spirit that was, is, and always will be. Our civilization awaits these higher forms of insight as a matter of life or death, for "Where there is no vision, the people perish" (Prov. 29:18).

On the Road to Higher Truth

A practical question will occur to anyone who has followed the preceding argument: What if—as may be expected—the vast majority of young people never attain any of these stages of higher knowledge during this life? What can they reasonably expect? Every young person who is guided *toward* the path of spiritual development will surely receive great gifts for engaging more satisfactorily in life. Much is attempted in this sense by Waldorf schools working with the educational insights and methods suggested by Steiner. The specific goal of these methods is to fulfill the true longings of modern youth by evoking and exercising the potential from which these longings arise.

Without reaching the initial stage of clairvoyance, which Steiner calls *Imagination* (with a capital *I*), young people's imagination may nevertheless be strengthened. As a result they will have a greater ability to enjoy life, because they begin to feel its pulse and power. From such awareness spring surprise and delight, refreshment and renewal. At the same time, disciplined imagination offers the ability to convert mere thought into practical energy and skill. The ability to transform abstract ideas into malleable *forces* overcomes the frustrating chasm that so often separates thought and action.

Without arriving at Inspiration, as Steiner understood it, youth can still be inspired to great effect. For example, right education can have the result that someone who is not at all clairvoyant will nevertheless be inspired through sleep. Such a person will awaken with good ideas, ideas that clarify the riddles of ordinary life and show the way to improvements and new ways of doing things—bold ideas that break out of the ruts of habit and custom. This ingenuity is incipient inspiration.

Where will we see evidence of progress toward Intuition? We will see it in the almost magical ability to *accomplish one's ideal.* Everything done deeply and permanently is done through grace. Grace attends the work of one who has placed self-will along side the will to do what is right and necessary. To live under grace is to have, as the meaning of one's life, an objective spiritual task. Anyone with such a task is granted the power to accomplish it—in spirit and in truth.

Every occupation, every profession, becomes real to the extent that it becomes a task of love. Teachers then actually lift and enable; they do not merely explain and correct. Preachers actually save; they do not merely exhort. Doctors actually heal; they do not merely medicate and perform operations. Marriage and parenthood, too, can become spiritual tasks, lived under grace. Then in the home there is warmth and health. These above all are the wish of every child and youth.

Considered that these three practical forms of higher cognitive forces amount to an ability to enjoy and contribute to life—to find meaning in existence, solve problems, and cheerfully persevere through adversities that would otherwise defeat the ordinary self. Such are the rewards of striving to make more room in one's heart for the mysterious Spirit that lives and rules through all.

2.

ON THE SOURCES
OF CREATIVITY

A Fact is the end or last issue of spirit.
Spirit hath life in itself. Spirit is the Creator.
— R. W. Emerson, "Nature"

EMERSON MADE A STRIKING CLAIM. What fires human creativeness, or chills it, he said, goes back simply to the way we as knowers approach facts: the objects, beings, and events that life sets before us. Creative energy begins to flow when in our contemplation of things we realize their origin in the spirit. He spoke of a draft of higher life found at that Origin, a "nectar" indispensable to creativeness. This true nectar of the gods, he said, is "*the ravishment of the intellect* (which is to say, the uplifting of human intelligence) *by coming nearer to the fact.*"

Do the kinds of observation and thinking that prevail today, not only in our schools and colleges, but in our civilization as a whole, bring us as human beings "nearer to the fact"? Or do they draw us *away* from the reality of the things, people, and events that we find ourselves trying to understand and cope with?

There are, indeed, two main kinds of observation and thought. One leads toward the spirit; the other leads away from it. Whereas both are legitimate and necessary, only "Spirit hath life in itself. Spirit is the Creator." To move toward the spirit, therefore, is to approach the ultimate source of creativity. On the other hand, to take pride in limiting oneself to "facts" as physically observed and intellectually interpreted in the usual way, undermines both the desire and the ability to create. Facts seen in this way are already created. They have reached the stage of materiality. They are creatures, and therefore no longer truly creative. Emerson calls them the "last issue" of creation—an end, therefore, not a beginning.

When fact issues from creative spirit and comes to the end of its road through physical manifestation, further travel in the same direction can lead only toward disintegration of one kind or another. The usual mode of investigation severs fact from its original lifeline to the spirit, so that it is left standing alone. There is no limit to the amount of dissection and analysis to which, as observers, we can subject facts. But their wholeness will always be divided thereby into subordinate parts and particles—on the way toward atomic dust, as it were. In losing their indivisible integrity, they will have lost the spirit that originally created them and still underlies them as their essential meaning. This is true of all natural phenomena, all beings and processes. It is most disastrously true of human beings.

Since we mean to focus here upon human creativeness, we are called upon to characterize in human terms what we mean by *spirit*. What is this spirit we presume to cite so boldly?

The less fearsome word *spirited* can help us here to keep our footing on firm ground. A spirited student is one who sits erect, with eager eyes, open ears, lively breath, and gladly beating heart—ready to learn, ready to do. His step has spring, and his pace alacrity. We can believe that whether he sits or runs, his internal juices will be coursing fluently, and his metabolism burning brightly.

Where does such spiritedness begin? What is the ultimate source of such an effective and desirable condition? In explaining, we greatly prefer to employ words like *interest, enthusiasm, affection, pleasure, hope*—anything to avoid the awkwardness, the public shame, of voicing the actually indicated word *spirit.* But spirit *includes* all these states of being and feeling that we would prefer to substitute for it. Let us use spiritedness, then, to designate in almost tangible terms the enlivening, energizing, creative power that spirit is. Absence of this power in a student, or in ourselves, shows itself as dullness, apathy, indolence—also as helplessness, depression, and fear. Every loss of spiritedness is at least a loss of creative power.

Narrowing our inquiry, we may ask: What accounts most essentially for the radical changes, from day to day—even from moment to moment—in the major condition we human beings experience as spiritedness? Does it not greatly depend on what we are *thinking*? It does depend on feelings, certainly, but don't feelings, for the most part, follow from thoughts—whether conscious or unconscious? Some thoughts are unnerving and life-quenching. They chill feeling and lame the will. Other thoughts have just the opposite effect. Is it not remarkable that something as intangible and, indeed, as immaterial as a single thought—a mere idea—can turn despair to hope, doubt to confidence, sorrow to joy, and even hate to love? Even a trace of changed *understanding* alters our whole mental outlook and emotional tone. In the process, it can also transform, down to the smallest detail, organic functions of the physical body.

Let us therefore not forget that a few centuries ago what we now tend to view skeptically and with a measure of contempt as "mere" ideas, were capitalized, even as we still capitalize God and Creator. Plato viewed Ideas as the archetypal Powers that build, sustain, and continue to inspire the manifest world. For him, what brings forth the physical rose is none other than the rose Being, the rose Nature, the rose Idea. For him, as for humanity in general in earlier times, Ideas were not the lifeless, helpless images seen in the mirror of reflective human brains. Ideas were the living, effectual presence of spiritual beings who stand *before* that mirror; or, as he said, they are denizens of the brilliant light realm shining outside the entrance to his famous cave (our human skull), who cast merely their shadows upon the rear wall within.

Thus, whereas brain-based ideas today can indeed be likened to such shadowy images, Ideas were once experienced as *self-existent,* creative identities, perceived spiritually. They were not only actual beings that visit or do not visit the brain, as birds perch or do not perch for a time on the branches of a tree; they were the outflowing, the progeny of divine Being Itself. The creativeness of real Ideas enters and works within the corporeal world but emanates from the higher planes beyond space and time we still call the "spiritual world." Because the Ideas, as inhabitants of this spiritual world, not only have meaning, but in and of themselves *are* meaning, it is from them alone that earthly existence receives the kind of meaning that is also creative power.

The riddle with which humanity is confronted, particularly by us today as parents and educators, may be stated as the question: How do we build a bridge from the world woven by physical sense-observations, as ordinarily understood, to the higher states of consciousness that touch creative spiritual actuality? This is the question we must address. The human heart, in its depth, requires this bridge from the *apparent* materiality of the world environment (which natural scientific thinking claims *is*, in the final analysis, indisputably material) to what nourishes enduring life and gives it meaning. How are the foundations of this bridge to be laid?

A second question necessarily follows: What will happen to the youth, as well as to those who are no longer young, when we fail to provide the necessary bridge sought by the healthy human heart? Does not this failure go far to explain the destructive trends in our society?

Human beings are born to enjoy life, divine its deeper meaning, and express themselves with creative love. In the beginning, according to the book of Genesis, the Godhead, or Elohim, said, "Let us make human beings in our own image." That is to say, Let us lift them above *created* beings, as the one who is uniquely gifted to understand, to love, and to create freely *anew*. But Genesis also tells us that human beings were destined to suffer temptations having to do with the quality of their knowing. Thus temptation was allowed to push them forward prematurely, while still unripe, in their appetite for knowledge. In yielding to this temptation, they would live in ever-increasing spiritual darkness and loneliness. Though fated still to feel passionate spiritual longing, they would find those longings obscure and thus be unable to achieve fulfillment. The aptitude for the divine creativeness human beings were destined to wield would find no proper outlet. Still present in the soul, but unrecognized, it could spend itself only in illusory adventures that would fail either to satisfy hearts or to fashion more than towers of Babel.

Following the same thought propensities that cast us out of Paradise long ago, we find ourselves today besieged by epidemics of alcoholism, drug abuse, pornography, criminal violence, environmental pollution, and warfare—to indicate only the conspicuously active side of the coin. The passive side of that same coin, however, represents an equal threat to the human community: intellectual apathy, emotional flatness, moral indifference, paralysis of will. We cast about in many directions for answers, though rarely in the right direction. Understandably, we look to church and school for basic help; but in our time, when religious faith has become anemic and education academic, religious preaching of "shoulds" and "shall nots" does not change human lives in their deeper motivation, and scholastic teaching of how to get ahead does not show students the way to fulfill their souls' true desires. Neither one gives them the power to master the thronging tempters that are in truth but unfulfilled, spiritual desire turned sick and ugly.

Because of the failure to strengthen the imaginative, inspirational, and intuitive faculties of the human soul to balance the purely intellectual, Emerson saw society wandering and stumbling into all kinds of blind alleys. And what he found dismaying in his own time 150 years ago has gone much farther in ours.

Emerson used a striking metaphor to convey his sense of what is going on in modern humanity. He reminded his hearers that there exists a "true nectar of the gods." It is precisely this nectar that is blindly sought now by human beings of all ages. The painful, half-conscious urgency felt by many among the youth of our day to discover who they are and what this earthly life is all about can be felt. And the disastrous consequences of their culture's failure to give them clear examples— or at least believable teaching—are equally apparent.

In his essay "The Poet," Emerson began by characterizing the special gifts and needs of the poetic or creative soul; but since all human beings bear something of this poetic soul in themselves, he soon passed from his focus upon "bards," to include "all men."

This is the reason why bards love wine, mead, narcotics, coffee, tea, opium, the fumes of sandalwood and tobacco, or whatever other procurers of animal exhilaration. All men avail themselves of such means as they can, to add this extraordinary power to their normal powers; and to this end they prize conversation, music, pictures, sculpture, dancing, theaters, traveling, war, mobs, fires, gaming, politics, or love, or science, or animal intoxication— which are several coarser or finer *quasi*-mechanical substitutes for *the true nectar, which is the ravishment of the intellect by coming nearer to the fact*. These are auxiliaries to the centrifugal tendency of a man, to his passage out into free space, and they help him to escape the custody of that body in which he is pent up, and of that jail-yard of individual relations in which he is enclosed.[1] (Emphasis added)

Emerson goes on to observe that because such substitutes for the true nectar are all "spurious mode[s] of obtaining freedom" and indeed "an emancipation not into the heavens but into the freedom of baser places," those who enjoy such substitutes are "punished for the advantage they won, by a dissipation and deterioration."

The presumably educated portion of humankind no longer knows how to develop the kinds of observation and thinking that draw us "nearer to the fact," nearer to "the nectar of the

---

1. Emerson, "The Poet."

gods that hath life in itself." To find again for youth the long-sought, indispensable draft of creative life must be the goal of all future education. Faith in the spirit, establishing faith both in the world order and in the essence of human selfhood, will restore to youth not only health and joy, but courage and creative will to solve the very problems presently multiplying beyond comprehension and control. Graduates of such new kinds of schools have every reason to look forward to lastingly, beautifully creative helpfulness in whatever field they eventually choose to enter.

3.

LIFE'S PURPOSE AND THE STRATEGY OF FREEDOM

A Letter at Commencement Time

DEAR YOUNG FRIEND,

I want to share some ideas with you at this dramatic stage of your life, and I wish to be somehow helpful and encouraging. Even as our civilization ends not only this eventful century and this extraordinary millennium, you, too, are coming to an end and facing the unknown. Will it be with confidence, or with "fear and trembling?" I assume that what you seek as this commencement launches you into a broader life is "The Purpose of It All."

Perhaps, more for my own sake than for yours, I feel a wish to review with you (age, confiding with love to youth!) some of what life has taught me about direction and attitudes in meeting life's sometimes ominous challenges. By being so bold, I must trust you to feel your way through my language, even when it gets complicated and philosophical—as I fear it will as I attempt, at the same time, to clarify my own mind.

Seeking "the purpose of it all" may be what even your parents are still doing sometimes. We observe that great nations, too, are engaged in this quest; the reason they find themselves floundering amid uncertainty is that they often find it difficult to find an appropriate purpose, and thus fail to pursue effective policies. The search for meaning and purpose starts early in all our lives; at your age it has no doubt been going on for some time. It seems more and more difficult to find the way, and the consequences of failing are increasingly severe for individuals as well as for nations; indeed, life's challenge can often seem grim.

Do I already hear an objection arising from your end? "I don't worry about the big Purpose. My concern is far more local and practical. Soon I'll be wanting a good job I can count on for a decent living. Even though that goal may still be in the future, it looms large in my mind. These days, it doesn't look good to me, and I haven't seen anything yet that makes me more hopeful."

I can certainly agree that there are the basics: the need to earn a living, and the less than prosperous outlook for the long road ahead. However, since the future course—at least on the larger scale—lies beyond us, I wonder if we are merely being compelled to find ways of understanding that will give us—within our small orbit and starting from where we find ourselves— some degree of control and some reason for confidence. I've found a few things I have found to be dependable, regardless of economic ups and downs, ways of viewing things that go beyond pious hope. They give reason for confidence, especially if the times get even more confused and threatening. Indeed, this very possibility has made me want to confide in you.

The outlook for a secure life becomes grim only when we get confused and begin to despair. Perhaps such confusion and despair result from the grievous feeling that in this difficult time we are single-handedly wrestling with the great mystery of life. Maybe the lonely struggle with oneself and with one's mysterious, uncontrollable environment cannot be avoided.

From one point of view, of course, we realize that it may even be desirable, since it can teach us certain lessons—especially, that the greater part of life's confusions and conflicts, as well as its fearsome qualities, may have less to do with the complexity or threat of the external situation than with the conditions in one's own soul, such as the negative thoughts and feelings we tend to nourish.

I suspect that we feel heavy and weak simply because we are weighed down by self-importance; we tend to grieve when our self-image has been slighted or the will blocked. At times, therefore, we wander in a self-invoked gloom. Our own small ego closes us off from the magnificent Sun, the everlasting stars, the beautiful Earth, and especially from the interest and love needed by our fellow-travelers. We shall not achieve fulfillment in life until this enigma of the personal ego has been solved; this ego usually makes too much of itself, but it should, in a different sense, make far more of itself. This self must come to experience the true Self, or "I," awaiting recognition. There is only one purpose in life that fulfills: the purpose freely fashioned and held before oneself.

One could ask: What do I want *most of all?* And this "I"— which is supposed to choose—is it the ordinary self or the true Self that knows the answer? Do I know who or what I really am? So often I seem to be in conflict with myself! How can I get a better idea of who I most *want* to become?

There are those who say there can be only one enduring purpose for our life on Earth. They say it is the one held by our Creator from Earth's beginning. Our only proper aim can be to *participate* knowingly, gladly, and creatively in the great flow of reality that wells forth from Divine Presence and Divine Purpose. Such people speak of God as the author of this mysterious adventure, life. If bringing forth the whole Creation was His choice and doing, then that choice and doing must still sustain the world. Independent-minded modern souls may therefore ask: How is our present human nature related to this primordial Creator?

Many of Emerson's writings faced exactly this question. His answers seem exceptionally revealing. His insights can help a modern mind—skeptical, yet willing to believe—if honesty permits it. We can try to understand what is going on in the whole world-evolution as somehow the expression of God's Word, a scripture bearing His signature, then Emerson reminds us that

> *Every scripture is to be interpreted by the same spirit which gave it forth....* [This] is the fundamental law of criticism.... The whole of nature is a metaphor of the human mind.... This relation between the mind and matter is in the will of God, and so is free to be known by all men. It appears to men, or it does not appear. [1]

This intuition led Emerson, while still a young man, to quote, in his first book *Nature,* his memory of the very congenial and recent affirmations that Amos Bronson Alcott had been making in their conversations together:

> The foundations of man are not in matter, but in spirit. But the element of spirit is eternity.... Man is the dwarf of himself. Once he was permeated and dissolved by spirit. He filled nature with his overflowing currents.... The laws of his nature, the periods of his actions, externalized themselves as day and night, the year and the seasons.

---

1. Emerson, "Nature."

But having made for himself this huge shell, his waters retired; he no longer fills the veins; he is shrunk to a drop. He sees that the structure still fits him, but fits him colossally. Say, rather, once it fitted him, now it corresponds to him from far and on high. He adores timidly his own work.... Yet sometimes he starts in his slumber, and wonders at himself and his house, and muses strangely at the resemblance betwixt him and it....

At present man applies to nature but half his force.... But when a faithful thinker, resolute to detach every object from personal relations and see it in the light of thought, shall, at the same time, kindle science with the fire of the holiest affections, then will God go forth anew into the creation....

The kingdom of man over nature, which cometh not with observation,—a dominion such as now is beyond his dream of God—he shall enter without more wonder than the blind man feels who is gradually restored to sight.[2]

Saint Paul said *"All things conspire for good, for them that love the Lord and seek to do his will."* He observed that such individuals find themselves aligned with the creativity of the Spirit that sustains and guides the universe. They therefore feel centered, secure, and at home with the miraculous world-process. Because they are close to the Source of being, they are by grace granted the insight and courage to move forward against all odds.

Dear Friend, as you've no doubt expected, I agree entirely with St. Paul. But I find myself therefore agreeing all the more when objections are raised to the way we call upon the name of God as our last word for explanation or proof, when most

---

2. Ibid.

of us have actually in mind only a being who is but our own, small ego's instinctive enlargement of itself. "God" in such case is Big Ego—"bigger," as a kindergarten child once ventured, "than the Empire State Building!" Perhaps this is the place to risk some of my own "I believe's."

For me, the bigness of God has no meaning until I sense it as indescribably beyond anything to be found in my *precious* little self. God's attributes are altogether beyond those that distinguish you and me from each other—especially the ones that tempt us to prefer ourselves. In respect of kinds and qualities, the Creator is not of any one or any other. Drawing upon His own creative, loving imagination, He made them *all*.

God is "Him in whom we live, and move, and have our being"—beyond the concept of space and time. Not far but near, not near but far, neither past nor future, but NOW forever. As Creator He is lofty beyond comparison, yet lowliest of all. Here on Earth, for example, He permits His handiwork to be heartlessly polluted, exploited, and exploded,—by the very beings He appears to have designed as the jewels and crown of His earthly creation. His will is absolute, yet every least one of us can ignore it and flaunt our defiance. His judgment is swift and sure, yet He seems almost infinitely patient with those to whom He gave His highest gift—freedom of choice, freedom of will—which is used to destroy one another and the rest of Earth's inhabitants. (The development of love, God's ultimate goal for humankind, would, of course, put a stop to such destructive behavior; but He, as Love itself, knows that real love cannot be mandated, installed or compelled from the outside even by Him. It can be offered only if and when it has been achieved as a matter of absolutely free insight and choice.)

If God has a name, I think it can be only the one He told to Moses from the burning bush: "I AM the I AM." (Exodus

3:14) This Name He alone could utter concerning Himself. Yet He gave of just this same, incredible essence to each of us human beings here on earth, that we might participate in the very source and heart of His creation, as ones who truly belong and who are central to its future. "Our Father" *allows* the temporary sacrilege of every small self referring so casually and carelessly to itself as "I"; but in our taking so trivially, so ignorantly, what should be the high reality of this "I," we distance ourselves from the creative, all-embracing love that is the reality of the divine I AM.

When I think of God, I cannot place or define Him in any way. I do sense Him as that Ever-Presence that knows and cares and helps, and whose loving Will be done, but this can occur only when we at last freely choose to obey it after recognizing it as our very own essence—our own heart's desire.

In each of us, as we occupy and use our bodies, there lives the "I Am" who continues our life's everlasting adventure through and beyond all seeming deaths. Thus, in our visibility there lives the invisible, and in our mortality the immortal. As immortals we antedate our many historical births and outlast our many deaths.

Once we see ourselves as essentially spiritual, we can readily imagine other very real but physically invisible beings, of both lower and higher condition than our human one: gnomes and fairies, angels and archangels, seraphim and cherubim. I think of all space, all objects, and all worlds as inhabited or watched over by such beings. Above, attending, and within all that appears around us as created "fact," there are always inspiring, enlivening, formative beings of spirit at work.

The idea of God, for me, brings together all of these invisible realities. Humanity, for example, comes to expression as many and various, yet more fundamentally it is *one*. I believe the world of spirits is also infinitely various and should be thought of as multiplicity; yet it should also, ever and again, be recognized and turned to as *one*. I think of the *essence* of *all* creative entities as *that which unites them*. As mentioned, when Moses was spoken to from the burning bush and wondered who it was that addressed him, he was told, "When your people ask, tell them: 'AM the I AM'—the origin and essence of what I intend for each of you to bear within yourselves!" I cannot think of a better way to conceive of the creative ONE-ness that lies still deeper than our separateness and diversity—the ONE that will yet unite us.

Dear friend, please take this lengthy digression as an affectionate effort toward softening the barrier many of your contemporaries raise against those who insist upon God as I do. In this I trust that you—even if more from kindness than from agreement—will excuse my simple wish to speak plainly what I believe. The same I shall certainly do with your reply, should it come. Let us, then, get back to what first stirred in me when I thought of your present celebration. Even though words such as *purpose* and names such as *God* must be used, allow me to sketch the picture that sheds genuine light and offers the only basis for sound life-strategies.

Returning now to the question of life's purpose in the grand, comprehensive sense, it is urgent that we ask: What about our small, *personal* purposes? Should we imagine ourselves being encouraged, or even allowed, in the great scheme of things, to pursue *separate* choices—those that appeal only to *oneself*? If we all did that, what would happen to the whole Earth, and the universe itself? When we, as billions of small separate entities, each "do my own thing," will not the harmony of the whole break down? If what we take to be our own desires and impulses so frequently contradict each other, what kind of chaos will result when all human beings find themselves at odds with one another? This war of "all against all," as it has been called, would certainly be a disaster, since not even the strongest can win.

Must we, then, surrender our own freely imagined and chosen purposes in order to get behind God's Grand Purpose? Must we abandon our persistent wish to become what is unique in us? We don't mean God any disrespect; at the same time it doesn't seem right to abdicate our feeling of moral responsibility to be ourselves—to make real choices, stand for them, and be creative on their behalf in our own new ways.

Perhaps you find yourself agreeing: What a dreary prospect, merely to follow the Creator's preordained round, however divine it is supposed to be! I had wished to contribute something quite original, unexpected, and characteristic of *me*, something achieved by me alone.

Please be reassured that, whereas I bear no good news for the self-will of our small egos, I will say nothing against the true instinct that makes each of us want to be his or her own self—an effectively unique, thoroughly creative human being. I am calling attention only to something most of us overlook, when I ask you to realize that the source of all the originality and the guarantor of all the real effectiveness to which any of us can aspire is greater than we can realistically imagine. Yet *we absolutely need access to this Source.* And because we absolutely *need* it, it is also what we actually most *want!*

Christ said that for a branch of the grapevine to have power to blossom and to bear fruit, it must first have a living source in the central trunk of the vine. If this all-important connection is too tentative or too weak, the branch will remain barren. If the connection through which the sap flows is blocked or ill-developed, such a branch will become useless, fit only for burning.

Something in each of our small egos wants to have everything start with *itself* and revolve around *itself*; it wants, as it were, to set up a whole new world of its own. But something else knows that this kind of thinking is the way not to creativity but to barrenness; not to abundance but to poverty; not to freedom in a congenial, interesting realm but to lonely imprisonment in the boring, limited, prison yard of the small self. The only way to self-actualization is—as the Austrian psychologist Viktor Frankl discovered by bitter experience in the concentration camps of World War II—through *self-transcendence*.

We do not really want to be turned back in upon ourselves. And, to be honest, we know perfectly well that we are not strong enough, wise enough, or for that matter caring enough to be made the hub of a universe all our own. When left to draw strictly upon our own resources, we show ourselves notably unresourceful. We realize that, in wisdom as in will-power, we tend to be both ignorant and weak. In fact, the times that bring us memorable pleasure and fulfillment occur when we forget ourselves completely in companionship with, and service to, those people and things outside ourselves for whom we awaken love.

We find lovable whatever is noble, kind, and true. It is natural and right that we go through life seeking to ally ourselves with these qualities wherever we find them. Following this spiritual instinct, we are led to the truly lovable. They are happiest who begin in this way to draw toward the center what *is* love: the Center of their own center. Seekers of this kind begin to sense the reality of the vine of which they are branches and, so sensing, open ever more gladly and fully to receive the flow of living sap that, through them, brings forth its flowers and fruit.

The Strategy of Freedom

Certainly one of the keenest desires each one of us has is for freedom. Freedom allows us to feel we have a chance to do something we really care about. Without it, we cannot make genuine choices concerning the purpose of our lives. It is equally true, of course, that unless we have chosen an abiding, fulfilling purpose for living (and for which we are even willing, if necessary, to die) freedom by itself will have no solid meaning. Nietzsche placed *purpose* first in his observation that "whoever has a *why* for which to live can learn to live with any kind of *how*."

When we are fully ourselves, when we live from the very center of our own being, we feel free. But this statement misleads those who fail to realize that their true center is not a small, interior something called the "ego." Rather, it is *one* with the great mystery that surrounds us in the wonder of the whole resplendent, resounding universe. It is also *one* with an equally wondrous mystery that reveals itself privately in the perfect stillness, the seeming emptiness, of our own inner being. The true self approaches from outside as well as from within—from loving contact with other people, things, and the course of events, and from secret promptings in the soul itself.

Human beings who allow themselves to be led by the small ego end up both frustrated and embittered. They are hardly welcome among their own peers. When small egos do the pushing, life becomes—and is now tending to become increasingly—the "war of all against all." We know this story only too well. But when people realize that, at the deepest level, their essential being is absolutely one with the essential reality of both cosmic nature and innermost human nature, a completely new story begins. A new life-strategy based upon an understanding of freedom emerges.

In knowing our true relation to divine wisdom and love, we recognize that it is our task in life to maintain creative interaction between two worlds: the world revealed from outside and the world revealed from within. We must be decisively grounded in both worlds. Then the pulse of reality begins to beat in our own breast. We feel the sap of healthy life. We become both securely rooted and ready to bring forth our divine, human best.

An anonymous saying states the matter in plain, though difficult words:

We human beings are free only to see and hear—
to accept what we see and obey what we hear.

We do best when we see and acknowledge things as they are without interference from subjective fear or desire. Clear awareness of the context in which we live is absolutely necessary for creative freedom.

We also do our best when we obey the prompting of our inner voice, though most of us fear to trust it, even when we realize its existence. This voice, or wordless prompting, answers our questions about the most fruitful ways we can live our lives and face the world. This silent voice speaks from eternity into time.

Here, too, however, personal preferences and biases only distort—if not entirely block—the message. The hidden, inner world of spirit sees and knows the secret of things as they are and should be in the moment, and it already knows what we most want to know. Its judgment cannot be improved upon, and should therefore be heeded if one wants to function in a genuinely creative and realistic way in the world. Yet it is most important that, at every step, we realize: *to follow the inwardly heard words of truth, justice, mercy, and love means obeying our very own heart's desire.* Such obedience is the other aspect of freedom: the one that opens to both understanding and empowerment.

Life is mastered through obedience. In this sense, Emerson spoke of "the gravitation of spirits" that forces us to look up to and move toward those whose obedience exceeds our own. Such individuals allow the warm, strong power of divine Presence to exert a gravitational attraction on us. Quite naturally, our soul orbits as a planet around such sun-power, in whomever it appears. Glad acceptance of life's *external* conditions, trusting obedience to the objective *inner* word, permit spiritual sunlight to work joyously outward from us.

When we hear and obey the ideal speaking so quietly from within (and we shall not hear it very well until we begin to trust it), and when we truly see and accept the world's events, we become at last the unique world stage upon which inner and outer world realities can interact for the good. Their interpenetration is exactly what brings us to living wisdom and heartfelt love, as well as to worthwhile achievement. In the freely balanced harmony of this procreative relationship between inner and outer reality, we find joyful fulfillment. Thus it can happen that, in the process of pursuing our *own* freely chosen and creatively managed purpose, we also play our destined role in *world* evolution.

Therefore, my encouraging advice to you, my friend, is not to struggle too hard with the course of external events. They are what they are, and somehow God's far-seeing loving wisdom is in them—despite appearances to the contrary. Strive only to recognize what *is*, without any bias of preferences or preconceptions. Judge not! Accept in a positive attitude, in good faith (gratefully, and with good hope) what life actually offers.

Do not struggle too hard with yourself, either. Modesty and confession are always appropriate, but too much remorse over one's impurities and inabilities can become no more than the shame of a self-occupied small ego that wants to be seen as perfect and great. Urgent efforts to reform faults and failings can sometimes betray only the conceit of an ego that would like only to prove to itself and to onlookers.

The right idea, I suggest, is neither to give in to the admittedly weak self, nor to fight it, but simply to look away from it toward what is high and true, real and kind. Let us look at our faults and accept them; for what else but faults can be expected of a monkey such as the little self when it becomes pretentious? Let us hear the thought-voice sounding in the heart and obey it, while realizing that not only can it speak the truth and know what must be done, but that behind it lies the only power that really cares.

Offering our plainly recognized faults, one may pray: "Dear God, though I am trying to be different, I admit that the disappointing imperfections You clearly see in me is the way I really am." Admitting that we don't know how our limited nature can ever enlarge itself through any amount of prideful striving, or how our stubborn self-concern will ever achieve love, we recognize that the cure for our own earthly limitations must lie in heaven's compassionate vastness. Without shame we admit it and ask help in not forgetting it. With all the greater trust and hope, we wish to obey the spirit's voice rather than what pretends to be our own.

As individuals, we become effective and free only when we become gladly active as agents of the universal spirit. When we do our best to act for God, He will act through us. This takes place only to the extent that we have subdued the pride of our own opinions and put aside the arrogance of our self-will.

Goethe said that to *"die and become"* is the strategy for life. He meant that we should cease to identify our eternal self with the bodily organism it inhabits. Before long, all bodies die; but the body's hold on our thinking and feeling should be surmounted during our earthly life. Should we not, then, live strongly and with due gratitude in this physical organism and let the soul in us stand free in self-recognition and control?

Of course, when the body-based ego is told it must die, it instinctively shudders at the verdict. How can we be enthusiastic about dying, especially when we are only beginning? Yet this "death" spells not confinement but release, not falling but rising, and certainly not the end of fun but the beginning of delight. When one has ceased agonizing for wisdom (recognizing oneself as unwise); striving for perfection (fully knowing one's imperfections); and currying admiration (admitting that one is not very admirable)—one embarks upon a new day, lighthearted and free. The painful effort to be what one is not, to do what one cannot do, subsides. One is free to step forth into God's world unburdened, expectant, unafraid.

Viktor Frankl made this prayer: "From the narrowness of my prison I called upon Thee, O my Lord, and Thou answeredst me from the freedom of space."[3]

---

3. Viktor Frankl, *Man's Search for Meaning*, Touchstone Books, New York, 1984.

As I bring all this unsolicited advice to an end, please allow me to mention a paradox that experience has taught me to value.

There are many times during our quest for the joy of right purpose and real freedom when life itself will seem especially joyless, even painful, ugly, and impossible. How can we deal with such times? Saints and sages have always given the same advice. I've found it again in *Turning*, a small volume of anonymously inspired words:

> Only when you are most low
> can you receive the highest.
> Only when you are most empty,
> can you be filled.
> Only when you are truly at rest,
> can I be active in you.[4]

What are we to do with this clue? Its positive focus is on our being "truly at rest," yet this comes immediately after the seeming negatives of lowness and emptiness have been also praised. On reflection, we realize that, when we are *not* "low" and "empty," we must be relatively high, and no doubt full— proud and full of ourselves. Whether or not we realize it, we harbor inner commotions or excitement that put us out of touch with who we are, what we want, and what needs to be done. We are unable either to hear the still voice of the Friend within, or to honor the wisdom of loving concern for our happiness. This message from *Turning* implies more than is immediately apparent. It suggests a way of dealing with life's disappointments, failures, and dead ends. We are called upon

---

4. Anonymous, *Turning*, Anthroposophic Press, Hudson, NY, 1994, p. 90.

to open our souls to a fresh influx of faith and hope—indeed, to bless this painful life and praise it as never before.

Intellectually we can object. We can wonder why. But semiconsciously we know the answer. When life floats us along too smoothly on the surface, it is easy to harbor illusions. On one hand, we begin to take ourselves too seriously, and on the other, to indulge our appetite for questionable pleasures. We tend to give our small self credit for our good fortune and entertain the unrealistic ambition—or the hope, at least—that our luck will last forever.

When, however, the conditions of life become impossible we are challenged directly to develop awareness of the real Way, real Truth, and real Life. We have to admit, at last, that we are not in charge but that a higher grace, known in the depths of our heart, that even now—especially now—waits patiently to comfort and inspire the soul.

> The other side of sorrow
> is joy.
> When you can raise your sorrow
> above bitterness, above disappointment,
> above pain,
> to the light —
> a birth occurs.
> In heaven the angels rejoice.
> Those who have died are fed,
> On earth the very soil is made new. [5]

Greeting the darkest days with a trusting, courageous mood permits us to accept cheerfully the conditions, both outside

---

5. Ibid., p. 91.

and within, that we ourselves cannot change. Above all, it opens our eyes to see the wonder and glory of the way life really works. When we lay our burden of false pride meekly upon the Lord, who rules without as within, He is free to do in us and through us the work that He knows (even as we secretly know) needs to be done. When our innermost self finds its way to this attitude, we are at last open to the experiences of both freedom and mastery. We know that somehow in us lives, and we live within, the invincible, world-creating "I AM."

Our Father in heaven, hallowed be Thy Name.

In this same name we, as genuine sons and daughters of our Father, at last find security, power, and unquenchable love of life.

I am not wise about life, but interested and enthusiastic! Even at my age, I am still keen on life and what is left of it for me. But to you, who surely have a fateful and adventurous future ahead of you, I can only say again: Have confidence in it; believe it is meaningful through and through. Gratefully enjoy the good, humbly contribute toward the redemption and healing of the bad.

4.

THE OPPORTUNITY
OF ADOLESCENCE

THE FULL REALITY of what in human life is called sex is grounded in the supernatural. So-called sex conceals the highest forces of the human soul: those of insight, love, and creative power. Many young people wonder why sexual activity should not begin as soon as the sex organs are ready. In the case of animals, sexual maturity soon leads to sexual functioning. In the case of human beings, however, biological readiness occurs ten or more years before marriage. Does this gap have a purpose? How should it be used?

It seems that true sexual readiness is achieved years later than physical development would suggest, and when sexual activity occurs before this time it leads to exploitation resulting in diminished vitality and longevity of function. Observation of life further suggests that young people who achieve a significant degree of sexual continence and sublimation are far happier and more active, healthy, and creative than those who take the allegedly natural path of yielding freely to sexual desire. More importantly, what youth does with sexual energy directly bears on the social future—the future toward which all people, but especially young people, should be looking.

If we are to have any hope of restoring freshness, beauty, and strength to humanity and to nature, an altogether new level of insight and power will be needed. The necessary forces will be available only to those young people who achieve a better understanding and make better use of the primordial life-function than their elders have done. The primary challenge to youth is presented by a deteriorating civilization; but the *power of renewal* that can meet that challenge has not yet been recognized. Thus, it is being squandered, and with it humankind's best hope for the future.

Cultural decline is a matter of eyes being closed, hearts hardened, and wills paralyzed. This decline began with the materialism that follows from intellectualism. Only intuition or imaginative vision can discover the ideals for which all human beings yearn. Awakened intuition overcomes materialism and opens the eyes of spirit.

Much of what we call sex in humankind today is not biological in origin but arises from disappointed or frustrated intuition. The purpose of education should be to strengthen and safeguard the intuitive nature, which in modern youth wants to be expressed as never before. But, in most schools, what is happening is typical of both materialism and the fight against materialism. On the one hand, there are great hopes for what could arise from a better understanding of the mystery of sex. Such well-intended hope lies behind the strong movement for sex education.

On the other hand, materialism keeps jealous watch over its own and has its own purposes for sex education. Through the rationales of modern biology, psychology, and sociology as applied to sex, materialism expects to win the decisive battle against the only adversary able to overthrow it. By treating sex as "perfectly natural," and by teaching means to reasonably use it for maximum gratification within the context of society, materialistic sex education effectively sabotages the very hope it pretends to be serving. Human sexuality, however, is essentially the most "unnatural" thing in all of human experience. Although it appears as an important phenomenon of nature's biological process—as a physical fact—like the iceberg, its greater part by far is unseen; most of human sexuality cannot be found in nature at all. The full reality of what is called sex in human life is grounded in the supernatural.

If we may say that there is a supernatural aspect to all natural phenomena—not just sex—it is still true that in sexuality the metaphysical reality predominates over the physical. In no other area will the sin be so great as in that of sex if the teacher's interpretation is not based on the spiritual secrets behind the physical facts. To materialize sexuality through sex education (as other phenomena of nature have been systematically materializing) is the worst possible mistake and will certainly have disastrous consequences, both individual and social.

There are many who feel that it is better to remain silent when, even though they sense the holy mystery of sex, they cannot set a shining example through mastery of it nor find adequate concepts in the repertoire of natural science with which to explain it. Perhaps it is safe to say that many parents and teachers are reticent about discussing sex with their children and that they hold back not out of ignorance of the facts of life nor from prudery, but because they sense that almost anything spoken from ordinary concepts on this subject—no matter how well intended—will fall short and may be misleading.

One who can speak in an illuminating way of sex must be wise indeed. One who can speak confidently of it must be a hero. One who can speak of it with purity is already a saint. Who thinks themselves wise? Who can boast sainthood? Fools rush in where angels fear to tread, and when the blind lead the blind, both fall into the ditch. Yet one cannot give up reminding young people of the transcendental possibilities of a force that is otherwise being squandered today because it is undervalued. The first steps can be taken only on the basis of a spiritual concept of the world, beginning with moral self-development; for sex is a spiritual force in the most immediate sense. So-called sex conceals the highest forces of the human soul—those of insight, love, and creative power. If these forces were recognized in education, youth would be on the path to overcoming materialism. If, however, they continue unrecognized, youth will destroy both itself and its rightful future.

A traditional ideal among Western civilizations has called for a serious effort toward continence throughout the period before marriage. Recent theory tends to discount this ideal as unworkable and perhaps harmful. If nature is ready, modern reasoning goes, it should have an acceptable and prompt outlet. Either masturbation or premarital intercourse, or both, should be regarded as wholesome. The arguments for early sexual activity, which pretend to be based on science and their logic, are well known and have a persuasive simplicity. And they contradict the much older, religiously-based traditions of Western culture. Where does the reality lie? It seems that the older traditions of sound human development through sexual continence were realistic and deeply wise, but we need to be reminded in modern terms of why this is so.

During the period between about twelve and twenty-four years of age, two powers in particular are released in the human being: those of the intellect and of sexuality. These powers are mysteriously related, yet they oppose each other. They confront each other as the higher and lower poles of human nature, and the tension between them develops everything that is best in humanity—indeed, everything that is characteristically human. This tension has the greatest potential for creativity; it should transform both sexuality and intellectuality and thus establish the *central* core of human nature from which proceeds mastery of both poles.

In order to understand the tension between intellect and sexuality, we must gain an idea of what each of these faculties represents psychologically. Sex is the blind will to combine in order to satisfy. Intellect, on the other hand, consciously pulls apart, in order to understand. Sex is warm attraction, whereas intellect is related to what youth today calls "cool"; it puts distance between people.

The mind's power for objective inspection must be strong enough to balance subjective sexual attraction, if both are to contribute toward love. Because sex has immeasurable depth and strength to attract and combine, so also the idealistic mind must be strong enough to discriminate, individualize, and hold apart. Thus, two main possibilities exist. These two forces can lay siege to one another so that both are entangled and crippled. In this case, the creative warmth of life is quenched by intellectualism, whereas clarity of intellect is darkened in turn by eroticism. The better possibility, however, would be that the poles of human nature approach each other with neither aggression nor submission but with *love*. Each pole will then sacrifice itself to experience the other; each will deny itself for the other's sake, expecting to have its life returned in a higher form.

In such an act of love, thinking waits until its abstract quality has been transformed into pictorial concreteness—its coldness into warmth, its aloofness into intimacy, and its desire to split parts out of wholes into the will to comprehend wholes in their indivisible, vivid unity. The corresponding act of love at the opposite pole induces sexuality to restrain its urge toward physical embrace in order to advance spiritual comprehension and to curb its compelling physical ardor—the immediacy of its appetite—for the sake of considered judgment and enduring insight. Sexuality that allows itself so to be mastered, and thus to die into its opposite, rediscovers itself as *intuitive love.*

In this way both mind and will are transformed by the pure power of feeling, whose organic basis is found centrally located between the upper and lower aspects of the body—in the heart.

There is a most favorable moment for the confrontation, interaction, and mysterious transformation we have described; this is the moment that began our present inquiry—the interval between early adolescence and the mid-twenties. During adolescence sexual vitality can most fruitfully be drawn upward to enrich the heart with pure feelings of every kind. Then, although physical desire may be strong, the germinal power of heartfelt idealism will also be very strong. When, however, desire is allowed physical expression before it has been transmuted into pure feeling, a precious possibility is foreclosed: the heart's possibility of growing larger and freer, gladder, and more creative in its central function. The soul loses hope for its highest aspiration—the chance to achieve a full measure of love.

Those who speak of a life according to nature and who speak of the naturalness of sex should remember that human nature at its best is by no means natural. Heretical though it sounds in these times, truly human capacities are in a real sense antinature. They are won by triumphs over natural instinct and impulse. Clear thinking, for example, requires the stilling of natural movement, and in this sense it is allied more closely with death than to life processes. Courage is the willingness to sacrifice one's natural clinging to life; endurance disregards natural fatigue; altruism ignores natural self-interest; objectivity checks natural bias. By the same token, love is born when natural sexuality sacrifices itself to become heroic idealism; and love is born again when the natural detachment of intellectuality is sacrificed for participatory consciousness.

Love is the wholesome marriage of body and mind, of will and thought. When the will sinks into materiality and condenses as a demand for premature bodily outlet, it becomes unavailable for true love. The bodily force of will then holds sway as a dark element below consciousness, as a crude element below refinement, and as a self-seeking element below compassion. This lower element that has failed to become fully human and has, in fact, become an abiding counterforce to true human nature will also create difficulties at the upper pole. There it will leave the abstract mind stranded, short of life, warmth, and power of realization. Such a mind is, in its own way, as great a threat to human welfare as is rampant sex. As Schiller pointed out, the latter makes the savage, the former, the barbarian. Between savagery and barbarism the cause of humanity is lost.

Children are able to make the most of their adolescence and early maturity if, during the elementary school period, all instruction has been directed to the heart. During these years an appropriate, articulate, vivid life of feeling—not sentimentality or any kind of sensualism—should be cultivated. Instruction at this time calls for thinking and for actions of all kinds to be done with love. Such a warm-hearted, artistically active approach to life will hold the powers of intellectuality and sexuality together long enough to transform each other; the adolescent youth can then mature as a balanced human being. If the young have been permitted long before adolescence to develop a capacity for vital, intimate *feeling*, then when adolescence begins their primary experience will not be the tormenting attack of sexuality but a powerful influx of interest and caring, of insight and creativeness. For them, the physical aspect of sex will be born more gently, gradually, and modestly. Intellectual power, on the other hand, will be born caring, imaginative, and intuitive. The two poles will remain in league rather than at war with one another. Both will serve the heart, where humanity has its throne.

The main problem for young people today is that they usually lack any real concept of the possibilities of human development. They may imagine that the purpose of life is to use their inherited or acquired powers to accomplish something in the *outer* world but not in themselves. It may never occur to them that their greatest task is to conceive and bring themselves to birth as creative, self-directing human beings. They hardly imagine that, long after physical conception and birth have brought them *externally* into existence, their continuing effort must be to evoke in freedom, and to patiently construct a whole being—their own—who will simply not exist if they proceed only according to the "natural" maturation of their given forces in the given environment.

Human beings are not naturally given their humanity but must individually and explicitly fight for it. This fight is against nature, to impose our will on nature, to take hold of nature and reshape it according to our own ideas. When we feel lazy, we make ourselves work. When we feel resentful, we try to forgive. When we want to run away, we elect to hold our ground. And when the body selfishly desires, we transmute this desire into objective interest, outgoing affection, and creative helpfulness.

If only young people could imagine what it means ideally to embrace the eternal masculine—the high daring and humble service, the instant decision and patient endurance, the fell attack and gentle succor, the fearless championing and compassionate shielding. If only young people could imagine the eternal feminine—drawing humankind ever forward and up toward beauty and romance, toward enlightenment and love, toward creativity and salvation. Yet neither the archetypal masculine nor the archetypal feminine is an attribute of birth— neither is given, both must be attained, and that is what the years between twelve and twenty-four are primarily for.

Sexual appetite as a merely physical imperative is a dragon confronting those who seek the treasure of full humanity. This dragon intervenes between the boy and his manhood, the girl and her womanhood. The dragon of sexuality can be disguised, embellished, romanticized, and allegedly tamed in many ways. It remains a dragon, a fatal enemy of higher human development. It is, of course, not sex itself that must be slain—that is, masculinity, femininity, and the power of procreation and sex as the *pure and blest* expression of loving hearts—but eroticism, amoral desire, impersonal lust, self-serving passion that must be eliminated. The phoenix that rises when the beast has been slain without mercy is a transcendent force like no other, a force that unlocks all doors, lifts burdens, lightens darkness, warms what is lonely and cold, gives strength to the weak, heals the sick, transforms ugliness to beauty.

In a 1966 lecture on Wagner's opera *Siegfried*, Franz Winkler said that the young hero gained three rewards when he slew the dragon. He acquired the ability to experience and understand the inner life of nature; he discovered his own task, or goal, in life; and he became able to find and recognize his true life's companion, Brunnhilde.[1]

It was Dr. Winkler's thesis that, by overcoming the dragon of erotic desire, Siegfried gained the power of intuition. First of all, intuition opened the secrets of nature to him, the language of beast and bird. Then, intuition showed him his own deepest nature and how it should relate to the needs of the world. And finally, intuition led him past illusory attractions to the loving soul of the woman meant for him.

Now a young person hearing all this might say: I am only mildly impressed. After all, what is being said? Siegfried becomes a nature-lover! He finds work! He discovers his woman! With any kind of luck, I hope to do the same. I already feel I can do that. Dragon-slaying is really unnecessary.

This, however, misses the point. Unable to break through the banality of ordinary concepts, such a young person would miss the extraordinary drama of the transcendent idea Wagner meant to convey. What is the significance, first of all, of the intuitive experience of nature as symbolized by Siegfried's sudden understanding of the language of the birds? This points far beyond the appreciation of most nature-lovers. This victor in the battle with the dragon comes to feel and understand creatures that are at first merely observed. He finds that he is related to all of nature's beings and events by ties of deepest sympathy and insight. The secrets that may be read in nature's living book bring him a gladdening, healing wisdom. As the human "I" awakens to the "Thou" of nature, the experience of nature becomes heartfelt *participation* in a divine drama. This brings catharsis and illumination to the soul.

---

1. Franz E. Winkler, *For Freedom Destined*, Waldorf Press, Garden City, NY, 1974, pp. 40-41.

Anyone, for whom opaque fact becomes luminous experience in this way, will be on the way toward the transformation of science. For when science can apprehend value and meaning, life and soul, as it now does weight and measure, the way will open to a completely new culture. We shall witness the renewal of agriculture, medicine, education, the economy, and social relationships.

From imaginative, inspired, intuitive forms of *science*, a new *art*, too, will inevitably flow. The creative powers of the cosmos will begin to work their wonders in and through human beings, sweeping aside all that is now trivial or perverse. Finally, in the culture where a new science, a new economy, and a new art begin to appear, religious experience will also be renewed. Not only will those who perceive the world in God live creative lives of wonder and praise, and not only will each learn the secret of human dignity through awakening to the divine in others, but every deed done will be a ritual and every material handled will be a sacrament.

Nothing slight is indicated by Siegfried's intuitive experience of nature, and the same must be said for his other two rewards for subduing the dragon. What does it mean to discover one's work? Certainly it does not mean simply to arrive at the idea that one will be a banker, lawyer, teacher, or entrepreneur. For one thing, no one who has the initiative, courage, and burning idealism to conquer the dragon of lower instincts will be content to settle for any of the usual slots of contemporary life. Such a person will probably have *ability* for many vocations, but none of them as such may seem either inevitable or fully satisfying.

The problem, therefore, does not consist of trying to see where one fits comfortably into the existing situation, but it is really a matter of becoming aware of one's own deep-seated, creative life-intention—the dream that makes existence worthwhile and gives it heartfelt purpose. One discovers work as a *calling* only when intuitive knowledge of the individual's most profound hopes is complemented by an equally vivid awareness of what external events require. Then, an earthly endeavor that is also a spiritual task will begin to develop, and life will begin to shape itself as a work of art. What reality ultimately demands is, at the same time, one's true heart's desire. This is the greatest fulfillment, and few achieve it. How productive, happy, and peaceful the world would be if only we could all work in this way.

To find the mate that one can love for a lifetime and throughout eternity also requires intuition. The deepest self-knowledge and self-activity is needed for an individual to discover the soul that matches his or her own. Until we sound our own clear note as individuals, we cannot develop an effective sonar for locating those who belong to us and to whom we belong. The same ability that discerns the spiritual in nature is needed to distinguish the lasting and true from illusory and passing desires in the soul. It is this intuition that sees the essential being of another and binds us to that being with enduring love.

Our most basic longing is not for sex as such but for uplifting happiness of soul. Sex in us does powerfully seek to vent itself; but when we understand ourselves, we truly want sex to fulfill its destined high purpose as the consummate expression of heartfelt love. Far too often physical sex is both a threat and a burden for the soul. Under the right conditions, however, it can serve as a perfect expression of love. When completely absorbed into what is higher, it then becomes, as it were, invisible. It is eclipsed in the heart's experience of pure joy. When the heart has awakened to love, the lower body is taken up chastely into a holy mystery; for true sexual love can be more chaste than troubled abstinence. To the degree, however, that thought and feeling allow the physical embrace to remain merely physical, happiness is clouded and fulfillment postponed. The ideal relationship of romantic love is achieved by only a few, but this fact makes it no less self-evident, desirable, and effective as an ideal.

Nowadays, for many people, *chastity* sounds "pure," but also "pale and cold," perhaps "good," but also "anemic" and "barren." Materialistic habits of thought make chastity seem like the impalement of a living being upon an abstract ideal. At best, chastity is regarded as a kind of suspended animation. Let us remember, however, that vegetative nature is chaste, and yet she produces fruitfully enough to be the very symbol of abundance. The growing, flowering, and fruiting kingdom of the plants is truly chaste; yet so creative, dynamic, and beautiful that all other living things find their sustenance in it as well as their enjoyment.

Praise of chastity must, of course, make youth look at parents and teachers and wonder. The young people must wonder, for example: What is it about marriage that allegedly sanctifies sexual activity? And they must wonder: Why—if parents were more or less continent in youth and now presumably sanctified in the matter of sex—are they still so often uninspired and uninspiring?

Youth's thinking will be sabotaged right from the start by one false assumption—that is, believing that the adults in charge of morality actually represent the path they claim to believe in. Youth tends to be idealistic concerning any matter about which it is uninformed, and it therefore generously imagines and hopefully supposes that most respected adults have kept pretty close to the straight and narrow in regard to sex. How, then, can these grown-ups be so uncaring toward nature and so generally uncreative and undiscerning toward their children? How can they be so unresourceful in dealing with the great problems facing humankind and so often petty and mean to each other?

Marriage, of course, does not sanctify sex. Impurity remains impure, and it has consequences within marriage just as it does outside it. Sexual activity is impure to the extent that it is not transformed, or transfigured, by love. Love is a high name for affection that is contrite, trusting, worshipful, courageous, magnanimous, rejoicing, and whatever else is needed to purge it of selfishness. Most marriages are not fortunate enough to be built on an adequate foundation of love. Most children are not conceived out of well-developed love, and they carry for life the resultant physical and psychological deficiencies and distortions. They are also likely to confront temptations from which they could have been saved.

A happy marriage means sunshine in the home. Sunshine is sweetness, clear light, and cheerful warmth. The reason so many marriages are not sunny is that the green of love never had the chance to mature before its further development was checked by physical expression through premature sexual activity. Love was never allowed and helped to establish its full power. It remained too tentative and weak to transform selfish desire into innocent happiness.

In most marriages, something is always left unredeemed, and this dark, unhappy element may well account for many of the qualities children object to in their parents—the dull clod syndrome as well as the anger and cruelty. Most simply stated, innocent love is true love and it guarantees sunshine in the home; but the aftermath of unleavened, or untempered, desire—both within and outside marriage—is darkness of mind and coldness of heart.

One may risk the generalization that marriage will be unhappy when the twelve or fourteen years before marriage failed fully to serve the purpose for which they were intended. Such a failure is typical in our time. Certainly many of the aspects of modern civilization that militate against love are now at their worst. Out of the very midst of this situation, however, something quite new and hopeful is springing up. This is a redoubled idealism among many young people—a will to change and be changed. It will bear fruit in the kind of love that makes either marriage or celibacy happy and fills life with blessing—*if* it does all it can during young manhood and womanhood to safeguard the magical power concealed in sex.

5.

LOVE AND THE
ILLUSION OF LOVE

EVERY SOUL LONGS for self-transcendence—for a loving share in the everlasting as found in the wide reaches of universal nature and in a deepened experience of other human beings. When this longing is frustrated—as it is in many modern souls—mind-changing drugs and erotic adventures may present themselves as enticing substitutes. But the soul that lets itself be fooled will find itself more self-bound than ever.

Those unaware of how the healthy soul draws light and strength from above are unable to weigh the pros and cons of behavior. Unless a person knows how spiritual powers are drawn down into and through the pure soul—protecting, encouraging, and illuminating it and all it encounters—one cannot adequately evaluate the traditional belief that unchecked sexuality is ruinous to the heart, will, and mind.

•

Youth can hardly be persuaded of the dangers of unleavened sexuality, because first caresses are so sweet. They are sweet because the innocence of childhood still imbues them. The caresses that follow are less sweet; innocence is progressively lost as physical contact becomes less heartfelt, and sexual appetite grows more aggressive. A hopeless quest begins in the attempt to regain what can be won only through renewed innocence.

•

There are some young people who sense the value of purity and want to walk that path, but may be unable to find a partner who will help, through their own steadfast modesty and discretion. There are also young people who feel the capacity and desire to be pure, yet find few companions who will, for the sake of this ideal, gladly subordinate their desire. Courage, chivalry, sensitive awareness, and purity of soul are the strengths of a young person's love.

•

One who loves life can never accept a negative ideal—gray theories that prohibit and paralyze. True ideals always speak for the affirmation and fulfillment of life—for the shape that integrated existence takes when it follows its own prompting.

•

Sexual passion in the limited sense becomes suffering inflicted on the soul by the body. It darkens seeing, deafens hearing, numbs touch, and paralyzes action. It blocks the way to what one really desires.

•

Although the sexual urge can arise from the depths of one's integrity as the pure and wholesome expression of love, too often it is actually an assault on the real self by an outside force. To yield to this assault is to accept servitude under a ruthless master.

•

Our time has been called one of "orgiastic impotence." The squandering of sex always leads to impotence of character as well as of the sex function itself. The result of sexual promiscuity and abuse is that human beings are losing control of their social and individual destinies and inviting various tyrants to rule them.

•

Sexual desire allows for three main possibilities: appeasement, repression, and transformation. Appeasing desire promises release from bodily torment but fastens the soul to the body's rack for further torment. Repression of desire, on the other hand, does not banish desire but spreads and deepens its invasion of body and soul. Desire is *mastered* only when thoroughly enlightened. Transforming desire evaporates it, releases it from the purely physical, and lifts it toward its primordial form as psychic energy and spiritual creativeness.

•

When people learn to live from the center of their being instead of from the top, they will again begin to feel and breathe freely. The outer world, too, will be able to breathe. The breath of the lungs and the blood of the heart know how to mix what is above with what is below in the right proportions. Proper feeling and breathing introduce peace, harmony, beauty, and refreshment into culture. Within nature it properly mixes warmth and cold, moisture and dryness, in the climate. Right feeling and breathing help earth, water, air, and warmth to combine properly in the humus of living soil. This vital soil, in turn, brings forth health, sustaining plants, animals, and human beings. Noxious and parasitical organisms are repelled by such health, dying out, as though by their own volition.

Victory in the inner life over passion—over anger, greed, and above all unrestrained sexuality—restores life to both nature and culture. Thus is Paradise regained.

What expelled humanity from Paradise in the first place? Was it not eating the fruit of the tree of knowledge? The inwardness, or intimate being of things, withdrew from the advance of the unholy intellect. As in the tale of Sleeping Beauty, the world went to sleep in relation to the human soul and began turning to stone.

Intellect not only enchanted external nature, but it also created "sexuality" to beleaguer and oppress the human soul. Sexuality, as a purely physical impulse, begins with intellect, and it is redeemed only insofar as intellect is redeemed. The sublimation of sex begins when the intellect opens to imagination, inspiration, and intuition, which brings the world back to life.

•

The pallor and shallowness of the intellectual mind craves to strengthen and deepen itself with the marrow of desire—but that living marrow is *spirit*, not sex.

•

Love transmuted downward from soul to body becomes unleavened sex. The amount of raw sexuality in a person is equal to the amount of possible love not yet experienced. What blocks love today? It is primarily the intellect's world of stone. When intellect lays its rock upon the human heart, sex becomes manic.

•

Love does not arise from the spiritualization of sex so much as sex results from the materialization of love. The sights and sounds of the natural world and the thoughts and realizations of the mental world *should* awaken love in the human heart. When they do not, a possibility dies. In dying it sinks to the next lower world; it is added to gross sexual appetite, the fatal craving that can never be satisfied on its own level.

•

If the force behind sex did not *belong* in a higher world, it could not be so completely lifted into that higher world. The original force is love, from which sex is derived. This is the secret of sublimation: the stream is helped to return to its source.

•

During adolescence, young people are moved by the power of sex, which resides in the lower body. This is the time when they should also be moved powerfully by ideas that originate in the upper being. The ideas opposite to the instinct of bodily procreation will be spiritually creative—ideas that look toward the birth and evolution of the higher self. Such ideas are at work in the ideals of romantic love, which encourage a young person to restrain desire in order to gain in strength of character and to seek moral beauty.

•

If one can truly love an ideal, one can also safely allow the soul to be inspired by sex. Without that love, sex will extinguish the soul's light. To "idealize" sex is not at all difficult, but to love ideas is hard. Therefore, youth must work mightily at the latter.

•

If one cannot love an idea, one cannot truly love his or her mate, because the real, lasting part of any human being is this ideal nature. One who cannot steadfastly love enduring truth can hardly be faithful in marriage. Faithful love of the ideal alone guarantees strength and loveliness in human beings.

•

What transforms a mere idea into a creative ideal? It is the secret power hidden behind sex. It is spiritual will.

•

The way to control emotions is through a focused choice of thoughts. No thought serves all circumstances. It is important to have many thoughts within the constellation of one's idealism from which to select. If one loses touch with the vitality of one concept, it may be replaced with another. Thus, control is maintained, each ideal in turn is strengthened, and creative idealism establishes its dominion.

•

The battle with temptation is immensely difficult, especially in our time. Ordinary idealism and will-power are not enough. Codes and rules are unavailing. Even hard experience often fails to teach the lessons of control.

Yet, theoretically the way to control is easy. It is simply a matter of holding exclusively to the alternative thought representing one's true desires. This thought becomes a protective light and creative life.

•

Any alternative thought, the simplest, if focused in one's attention, has absolute power to vaporize the strongest desire. But that thought must in fact be preferred. Often one is more willing to wrestle heroically with the temptations of sex and lose regularly, than to hold decisively in mind the alternative that might end the contest.

•

One wants to love another? But is this possible? It may be difficulty at first, since real love is an achievement and doesn't just happen. It begins with a love of life, nature, beauty, and duty; it begins with true friendship.

•

When a young person is powerfully attracted to another, he or she has "fallen in love." Such a person may ask: Is this true love? The answer should be based not on the strength of the attraction but on its quality; compulsive longing always leads away from freedom. Too many young people marry because of such obsession and compulsion, because they "cannot live without" each other. Only *free* beings can offer true love.

•

During courtship, young people who hope to develop true love for each other should consider the following. In the physical world, we must reach out for what we want; there is no other way to bring it near. In the world of *inner* truth, however, things are reversed: what is reached for retreats; what is foregone approaches. Desire repels, for in desire the self presses its claim and thus obscures the thing desired, making it less available. Love, on the other hand, attracts. Through love self forgets the self and abandons all claims. The revered life of the other grows more vivid, more real, and seems to draw nearer; therefore the self finds itself ever more intimately united with this other life. Emerson stated in simplest form the gain through love, the loss through desire: "That which we love we have, but by desire we bereave ourselves of the love."[1]

•

The counterforce called chastity aims to help desire become love. Premarital chastity seeks to perfect desire so that love may be born in marriage, and the offspring born from love.

•

When young people realize that they will become parents, and if they consider the weight of such responsibility if their own children are weak or perverse, and how blessed if their children are upright, harmonious, and sound, they might prepare for parenthood with a fierce idealism. If young people can fully appreciate what it means to say with Novalis: "The child is a love become visible," they will also know why it is important to satisfy the rigorous conditions for thoroughly ideal friendship and affection.

---

1. Emerson, "Self Reliance."

In order to work with full energy for virtue, boys and girls need to see the requirements of an objective spiritual task such as parenthood and how early sexual activity clouds the vision and imagination needed for such a task.

•

Whereas the outer world of culture and nature has become prosaic and mechanical, humanity's inner world finds itself in tumult, filled with desire and raging impulses. Because of our materialistic thinking in terms of both self and world, too much of creative love is dammed up within. Too little reaches fulfillment through transformation of the outer scene through deeds of truth, beauty, and love. The inner fire, if tended and lovingly applied, can melt the outer ice; but when this fire is misconceived as a mere pleasure-principle and allowed to burn itself out selfishly, the world's ice thickens.

•

Desire burns solely for its object; it is cold toward everything else in the world. How great a coldness is purely sexual desire, whereas love is the flame that gives warmth and light to all. Sheer desire is love reversed—it subtracts from both warmth and light.

•

When we are colder toward what clamors to assert itself within us, we are warmer toward all that is presently cold, forlorn, and friendless outside.

•

Countless boys and girls, men and women, are unnecessarily lonely today because others, or they themselves, are locked in selfish desire. Nature, too, is lonely because humanity is too preoccupied with greeds and desires to share in her wonders of beauty and power.

•

The individuals in every adolescent couple either try to hold the physical expression of their developing relationship within strict limits so that it may ripen in the soul and bear fruit in happiness later on, or else they press toward early union because they cannot resist the magnetic force drawing them together. In the first instance, they experience momentary loneliness and lasting happiness, and in the second, momentary satisfaction and lasting disappointment.

•

Resisting sexual infatuation may feel like abandonment of one's very ego, emptying the soul of a precious substance. This seems like death. Yet magical powers of blessing sing and love attends those who can understand and make this sacrifice. This is the act that transforms planet to sun, awakening the god in human nature.

•

Willingly accepted loneliness can be a screen held by the courageous soul against false warmth and light.

•

One who knows how to love loneliness knows how to love humanity, nature, and God. At the right moment, the lonely who persevere find the dark night of their loneliness all warmth and light. As Saint Francis praised poverty, let us praise loneliness: Blessed be nothing, for it alone assures everything!

•

To praise loneliness is only a manner of speaking. It is not, in itself, a virtue, for to feel lonely is to remember the cause of loneliness, to long for the object of desire. Virtue works only when personal loneliness has been sacrificed to a vital interest in the objective world outside desire. That is when the new life, the higher life, begins.

•

To be lonely is to live in the past or future. Therefore, what banishes cloying loneliness is presence of mind. The smallest objective observation or immediate appreciation can instantly dispel subjective loneliness. But does the soul want it dispelled? Loneliness asks the heart in its depths what it really wants.

•

As a station along the way from subjective desire to objective love, loneliness can be a purgatory—a vacuum that sucks up egoism.

•

The love of two who are equally at home in loneliness will last forever.

•

A community that endures in loving kindness rests not upon instinctive congeniality among its members, but upon the compassionate will of those within it who are well-grounded in loneliness.

•

The human being is erotic; animals are not. The difference is intellect. Intellect creates impure eroticism and the physical enterprise called sex. For animals in the natural state, sex does not exist as a thing. It is a compulsive cloud of unknowing— innocent through unknowing and limited in its times and dimensions. Human sexuality is not limited to seasons, to a particular manner of fulfillment, or in degree. It is open to complete disorder. The cosmos itself orders this power in animals, but humanity in its will to freedom has wrested control from the cosmos. We are not presently equal to this task. Without divine help we have neither the insight nor the power to bring complete wholesomeness into sex.

•

Animals are attracted only to their own species. Human beings can be attracted by almost any object, animate or inanimate. But animals are limited by the wisdom contained in the instincts of their own kind. We can become wisely helpful to *all* kingdoms, but first we must overcome the ignorant lustfulness that works to destroy both self and world.

•

Chastity is love of spiritual life and faithfulness to the spirit. From this point of view, materialistic perception and thought are fundamentally unchaste; they lay the world bare. For the chaste soul, the world regains its modesty. All things resume their aura, which contains their life, soul, and spirit.

•

To render something chaste is to clothe it in spirit. Modesty veils itself not with shame but with sacred beauty and power.

•

Not the flesh itself, but what veils or permeates flesh awakens the heart and satisfies it.

•

Listen to the heart. It knows that the way to more intimate union is through modesty; that the mystery of approaching more closely lies in holding distance; that tenderness presupposes rigor.

•

Emerson hinted the principle of chastity when he said of the stars: "The rays from those heavenly orbs will separate between a man and what he touches" ("Nature"). Later he said that every object, when regarded properly, or when seen with spiritual eyes, has the same chastening effect.

•

Purity makes glad contact. Purity and a heart of delight are the same. Promiscuity ensures estrangement—an ever-questing, ever-deepening loneliness.

•

Chastity maintains as inwardness what belongs within. Free sexuality spends this inward power externally. Thus begins disintegration of the human personality. Unless checked and reversed, it will continue until every fiber of one's being is eventually torn apart, until the whole physical body has been reduced to atoms of unquenchable desire. If passion is suffering, this will become hell itself.

•

Mind alone cannot protect itself from impurity. Only the mind that speaks from the heart masters passion.

•

One who is content to remain a "normal" modern intellectual, or materialist, will not make much progress with chastity. Such chastity will tend to become frozen outside and violent within. The end is equally bad, however, when the erotic impulse is lived out, for it leads only to impotent despair.

•

When sex is one's basic inspiration, innumerable illusions prevail—illusions that distort facts, impair logic, dissolve commitments, and melt resolve. For this reason it may be said that objective spiritual tasks in life will surely find, use, and bless the young person, or any person—no matter what the station or talents—whose heart and will imposes clarity, correctness, and common sense upon sex.

•

Those who strive for purity of heart will receive the needed power—as both the armor and the weapon—in the battles on the long, slow road that leads humankind from slavery of soul to freedom, from darkness to light.

•

Doors of granite are closed today against the wisdom humanity needs for its own welfare and that of the planet for which humankind is responsible. Only one force is strong enough to open these doors: the force that longs to be redeemed from misconceived, misused sex.

6.

PERMISSIVENESS, DISCIPLINE, AND LOVE

THE SECRET OF DISCIPLINING children lies in the self-discipline of parents and teachers. In recent years, however, parents have been permissive as never before. They do not discipline their children, for fear of destroying initiative, spoiling pleasure, or incurring resentment. In any case, these are some of the reasons given. Regardless of any other reasons, parents are easy on their children primarily because they want their children to be easy on them.

We face a paradox; on the one hand, parents are trying as never before to cater to children, and on the other, children are more critical than ever toward their parents. Does this second fact somehow directly relate to the first?

We must moderate the way we "love" our children, if we wish our tribulations with them to be moderate. By not indulging temporary feelings of fondness, we reinforce the *enduring* strength of real love, which alone proves effective in time of need. The price of parental indulgence in good moments is estrangement in the bad moments.

Parents who would like to master their own anger and overcome estrangement when a child behaves badly, cannot find
such power in themselves unless they have previously stored it
there. They can store it by forbearing the nurturing of pride—
whether in gratification or in hurt—for through a proper
reserve in our attitude we create reserves of strength.

We should strictly watch the self-indulgent pleasure we may
be inclined to take in the accomplishments of our offspring.
For then we may also expect to be struck less personally by
their shortcomings when these appear. If apparent goodness is
not allowed to melt our hearts prematurely, then apparent
badness will not harden them too hastily.

The more we love our children, the more rigorously we
should be able to hold them to what is right. We love them
truly when we love what is objectively true and good in them.
Then, when the time comes to discipline them, we can do it in
the name of their own best nature. If our love is cold, however,
and we fail to see through to the spiritual, we are inclined to
become indulgent. We indulge our children both because we
do not care enough to do battle and because we seek to hide
our lack of caring under the illusory warmth of permissiveness.

Permissive parents have a hidden inability to care enough to
rouse and hold themselves to discipline, which in turn weakens
the moral fiber of their children. Parental indulgence leaves
children prey to unworthy cravings and fears. No child is more
insecure and dissatisfied than the one who has been catered to,
and none has a more dubious prospect of achieving what he or
she really wants in life.

The experience of parental discipline prepares a child for
successful self-discipline in years to come. The grown person
can more readily accept the guidance of the "still small voice

within" if during early years they had the good fortune to be guided by the firm conviction of strong parents. They will not find themselves as adults making the rueful excuse, "the spirit is willing, but the flesh is weak." Parental discipline prepares a *Dualism* child's own higher self to one day take command of the flesh. Permissiveness, on the other hand, strengthens the flesh in opposing the spirit later on.

Many parents give in to their children for fear of breaking their will. But how is human will really broken? It may be paralyzed by fear or rendered hopeless by frustration; more often, however, it is disintegrated in childhood through a lack of loving discipline. Strong-minded parents will generally raise children of strong character, for strength of will is contagious; it is imitated unconsciously during the first stage of childhood and consciously admired and adopted later.

Parents who impose their will in an absolute manner will more likely face the problem of offspring who are resistant to guidance from anyone with less force than their own. This, at least, is not a broken will. Parents who want their child to become tactful and amenable as well as strong, should cultivate in themselves the habit of being more agreeable, or flexible, in their own adult relationships.

Anyone who accepts the discipline of ideal standards and attempts to bring one's own behavior into line with what is true, beautiful, and good, is in a better position when called on to discipline others. Thoughts are then just and impulses objective; both will be accepted as no personal criticism or guidance could ever be. The secret is that what is personal in me is foreign to you, but what is objective and ideal in me is near to you. When one has been severe with oneself first, even gentleness and lenience with others have the effect of strength.

The disciplined individual does not speak from prejudice, fear, or desire. Such a person speaks for the uncorrupted nature of all people, and their speech is simply good sense.

It is hard, of course, for grown-ups to criticize or discipline themselves. After all, they have passed through the whole series of apprenticeships that school and the early years of vocation demand of everyone, and they have at last carved their niche. Although the images for mother and father are different in details, they are the same in essence; in adulthood, both feel they have arrived.

Continuing self-discipline, however, means that all the accomplishments of adulthood should weigh very little in our opinion of ourselves. Freshman year must be started all over again—and again and again. As "somebody," we must recognize every day afresh that we are "nobody" insofar as reality is concerned. Though we have the jingle of money in our pockets, we must admit that we lack the treasures gathered only by sympathy and love. Though we wield power in the world, we must see how we are powerless when it comes to achieving what is most desirable in ourselves and in others. Despite worldly experience, we must realize how far we are from experiencing the deeper truths of life.

As we gravitate toward the materialistic comforts of middle-age, we lose the inclination and courage to rise above and see ourselves from outside. We then fall under the illusion that we are the "haves." But when we hold to the self-criticism and self-improvement that we demand of youth, we are reminded of how much we are the "have nots." Through being able to see ourselves as others see us, pride is continually melted down and refined. All this painful crushing and smelting actually endears us to everyone—even our own children.

. . . .

The influence of a parent or teacher works in various ways on children, depending on their ages, yet the fact remains: anyone who would influence others for the better must first improve oneself.

Picture the situation of preschool children. They exactly imitate the gestures they encounter around them. Their imitation expresses the devout surrender—with no trace of criticism or restraint—of a small child's will into the hands of the parents. According to Rudolf Steiner, a baby's growing physical organism is subtly sculpted by the parents' characteristic voice, glance, gestures, and bearing.

In the elementary schoolchild, admiration, trust, and belief may be awakened, just as in a true disciple; both are filled with faith and feeling. Rudolf Steiner described the life-forces at this stage of childhood and how they are placed in the hands of parents and teachers—how the psychological behavior of adults has a great effect on the child. The future health and life-habits of children at this stage are shaped by the quality of the *feelings* they absorb from their parents—whether creative or apathetic, flexible or stubborn, radiant or depressed.

At adolescence, the ties of believing are loosened. Attachment now is to the *ideal* rather than to individuals. Because of this, youth is easily alienated from the actual personalities of parents and teachers. Young people still long to believe, but those who are available seldom prove worthy of belief. Until young people learn compassion for such mortals, they are often suspicious and cruelly critical.

Adolescents find their parents unworthy for what seem to be the slightest reasons. A characteristic mannerism, tone of voice, or attitude in parents may turn their heart to stone and their will into fiery opposition. For adolescents, seeming trivialities are not trivial but clear evidence of bigoted, sterile, untrue, or otherwise objectionable elements in the parents' thought and feeling. The least hint of such elements in their manner reminds young people of all they have suffered from the character behind the manner. Their own intimacy with this unwanted trait makes youth reject it even more violently.

All this youthful disappointment is natural and inevitable only when parents insist on viewing themselves as the accredited representatives of right thought, sound conduct, and good character. Youth's disagreement with parents will thus be fundamental and almost absolute. Let us not imagine that disagreement springs up only between ourselves and our adolescent children. Does it not still divide us also as adults from our own parents? The same rejection of parents continues throughout life and constitutes a major part of what we know in our time as the problem of unwanted, uninvited, unwise old age.

What can be done to ensure that a helpful influence may continue to flow from maturity to youth? Age must take the young path—the path of continual learning, of being continually corrected, disciplined, and humbled, being a freshman again every few years, days, or minutes.

One way to see the problem, therefore, is this: As we age, we petrify. And, even though we cease to improve, we foolishly insist on making our imperfect but hardened will prevail; this is where our children's resistance begins. To melt the opposition they offer us, we must melt the opposition offered by our own "natural" self to our own better potentials. We must remain pliable within. We are pliable when the universal spirit predominates in us, holding our character subject, preventing it from hardening. This higher nature is, after all, our own true nature and equally that of our children. Through being alert, impressionable, and attentive to the criticism inflicted on us by intuitive ideals, through being willing and courageous in changing ourselves, is to overcome the heaviness of middle-age, to become young again, and to command the respect of youth.

· · · · · · ·

Almost all children are difficult to reason with. Either they don't hear—as it often seems—or they don't take heed. This is to be expected, after all, since the tiny ones *cannot* yet understand, older children seem to be allergic to understanding, and adolescents have their own understanding of matters.

Little tots do as they see done. They are more or less immune to reasoning. Healthy children of the elementary school age, on the other hand, find reasoning itself to be somehow sick. For them, dramatic images are far more congenial and persuasive than reason. And high school youth are often simply contrary in their reasoning. They delight in rationality, but often use it primarily to support their own prejudices. Adolescents like to feel the cutting power of reason on someone else; only gradually do they gain the courage to place their own behavior under the knife.

Adolescents look you in the eye fleetingly, and if the "you" seen is too pedantic or personal, they are alienated and turn away. They might prefer that you looked through them rather than at them. But the adolescent rejoices to see in you a modest common sense, a gift of humor, some rapport and success with the objective world—over all, a sense for what stands higher. That adolescent's eyes will seek yours again and may trust your advice.

Many parents associate discipline with anger. When a child misbehaves or fails in some way, parents become angry. Things go awry and anger flares. Why is this?

Some of us are more prone to anger than others; there are violent natures and placid natures. But when it comes to our own children, even the placid often find themselves at the edge of violence. Generally speaking, we become angry when we are too weak to cope with a situation. Anger is an attempt to increase our strength. If anger carries us through the obstacle, we cool readily; but if not, a towering rage may develop. Despite its creative potential, unalloyed anger is destructive and must be checked. A good technique for parents is to remind themselves, when their children's weaknesses make them angry, that blind anger betrays weakness in the parent, too.

Anger is a creative power, containing both warmth and strength. But it is also blind. It is a giant who needs eyes. A giant, when given bright eyes, tends to diminish drastically in size; for it is well known that the clever tailors who see and reckon so well, and can often get the best of giants, are extremely small. So the clever little tailor, who also lacks something, also cannot be our ideal. Is it not the fire of *caring*, so closely related to anger, that would give the tailor stature and release from such scheming smallness?

The person parents and educators strive to be is neither the blind giant nor the clever little schemer, but someone who has balanced the looming power of anger with the condensation of thought, thus achieving a steady, ordinary size; such a person has tempered fire with ice and ice with fire to achieve the creative warmth of love.

Part of worldly wisdom is the realization that few people ever fundamentally change themselves. Yet we must change at least some basic weakness into strength if we wish to help others with their problems. Good discipline always starts with self-discipline.

The power we may already possess to discipline others indicates how well, up to this moment, we have already learned to control our own nature. When we need *more* power, we can win it only through further self-conquest. When the immediate matter of discipline will not yield to our best efforts—for example when we fail to bring our children beyond some basic weakness—the answer remains the same: We must somehow lay hold of more love, greater insight, stronger will-power. Our own growth in these qualities results only from further struggle to know and to change ourselves.

Most problems in life are caused by one's own shortcomings. This may be easy to see in other people, but it is not easy to do anything helpful about it. What we need is a method of *enabling* those we cherish, and for whom we feel responsible, to make the changes we so comfortably point out. The only method that is equally well adapted to all ages and allows their freedom, one that avoids nagging and actually generates the necessary power, is for us—inspired by either love or shame—to tackle our own weaknesses at a deeper level than ever before and to win.

Our disciplinary influence on children, as with others, is strongest when it is a reflex of successful self-discipline. As a reflex action it is always ready and prompt. This immediacy is a great advantage, since discipline that is delayed (even by a few seconds) starts badly. Reflex action also has an impersonal quality, which is good, since it is not aimed at anyone too directly, but is matter-of-fact. Further, because it does not stem only from ideas but from *character*, it has impact, consistency, and endurance.

The reflex of self-discipline exerts influence without making a major project of every disciplinary action. This means that we do not spoil the child in the very act of guidance as we do when disciplinary situations concentrate too much of the parents' attention and effort on each particular.

Self-improvement for the sake of others is *creative* in the truest sense of the word. By bringing to ascendancy in ourselves the supernatural power that makes mere men and women into true human beings, we add to the sum of existence. We introduce something fresh into the natural world. This power brings new things to pass, both in and through us. Just as the sunlight streaming through the window rejoices not only the one who opened the shutters but everyone in the room, so also the creative power of the spirit is by no means restricted to the individual who summons it.

Physicians do not heal directly through their own efforts; they arrange things so that nature can heal. The educator does similarly. By self-education the teacher becomes a channel through which the primordial human spirit may flow to accomplish its work in other lives.

What ultimately changes people? Do we not change ourselves? And what enables us to change ourselves? Is it not an influx of spiritual life? The whole Earth is enriched when any one of us reaches beyond our "given" nature to draw new strength from above. We draw strength from above by inviting and allowing it through the harmony we strive to develop in ourselves—that harmonious accord between an open mind and a ready will. This harmony attracts a higher power. The grace that comes does not belong to the person; its blessing is efficacious *beyond* the personal strength or wisdom of the one who chooses to be its instrument.

This kind of spiritual power is *public* power, though invoked by the private self-education of an individual. The whole human race is ennobled by its triumph in any individual.

When, for example, the radiance of spirit is seen in a neighbor's humble gratitude toward life, all our hearts are softened. Such humility causes us to forsake the egoistic structure that has been our platform and our barricade and makes us realize the unloveliness of our own criticism. And if the ideal power is manifested by a certain heroic striving, we are all inflamed with the passion to master our circumstances.

Parents, teachers, or statesmen who want to help others improve need at least three things:

First, *they need expertise born of insight.* Insight into other human souls is gained to the extent that we learn to view our own soul objectively. But objectivity toward ourselves results less from so-called objective study than from subjective striving. Our first inkling of the ideal must be acted upon if we expect the ideal to reveal itself to us still more perfectly. When we *act* on what we have seen, our seeing is further clarified. After some degree of success in removing a fault, discovered perhaps by vague feeling, the causes and consequences will come into view. The eye that has been opened by self-knowledge—which follows self-conquest—sees remarkably well through veils that still hide some truths about themselves from good friends and neighbors.

Second, *they need the healing, helping power of compassion.* When we have taken the path that leads from the recognition of superficial faults in ourselves to surveying the deeper roots of our perverse behavior, we begin to develop compassion for the failings of others. Nothing checks criticism as surely as the lightning bolt of self-knowledge. When this bolt splits the cruel rock of pride, a healing spring is released—the water of pity and forgiveness. The flash of the ideal strikes us again and again; it illuminates the badlands of our inner landscape, and burns us at the same time with the fire of contrition. The pain we experience on our own account becomes tenderness toward others; the burning fire is transformed into the warmth of a just understanding.

Third, *they need the moving force of will*. What both adults and children need for help in overcoming difficulties is not analysis so much as *stimulus*. Very little reasoning is enough to indicate the nature of the necessary task, but a great deal of creative power is required when we actually do it. We cannot generate this power ourselves, however, when we speak as parents merely from the status quo in ourselves. Only when lifting oneself by the bootstraps can one usefully advise another. As Emerson said: "Do the deed and you shall have the power." The word of one who has fundamentally changed is mysteriously charged; whoever hears such a word is not merely instructed but enabled.

. . . .

One who starts from a strong feeling of selfhood finds that self-reform converges toward one goal: *humility*. If we can stand the insight, and if we have the appetite for it, fate will see that we are clearly shown our own powerlessness and deep inadequacy. Yet the confession that brings us down in our own eyes is the most encouraging thing in the world to others. It helps them to see the truth about themselves, because they can suddenly admit what they have always known.

As we begin to acknowledge the painful truth about ourselves, power from the higher world begins to work through us. Within our hearts it appears as joy and courage. In the outer world, its efficacy is manifested as a miraculous ordering of events. When humility stills in us the desire to moralize, censure, and exhort, it permits greater, more objective, and more skillful forces to work.

Children are far from being as recalcitrant as they seem. They want to admire us, heed us, follow us. We ourselves introduce confusion, disillusionment, and negativism into their lives. If we look at matters from their viewpoint, we see how much they feel the need to succeed in life, how they want to live fully, happily, and nobly, and how greatly they desire our help.

Children at birth bear something of the mother and something of the father (and the two natures seem to be mingled in such a way that the parents are confounded later on). In an instinctive sort of way, mother and father set out to educate their young ones, acting according to their own natures and using their natural instincts and abilities. For awhile they accomplish a good deal in this manner, since what one parent cannot give, the other often can. Thus, the children grow and improve. But they no doubt remain far from perfect. After father and mother have done the best they can with their given abilities, the children will probably continue to exhibit shortcomings that justify concern; specifically, they will show new variations of the same faults that have beset their parents all their lives.

A situation now arises that parents may think calls for discipline. But one thing is sure: children will not be improved by means of the same old treatment from the same old parents, if they merely continue to use the same approach according to nature and habit. After the typical stage of passive or active resistance has been reached, everything depends on whether or not the parents understand that, whereas their native, habitual virtues may continue to be somewhat effective in a sustaining role, one must expect that they will diminish in effect.

It is truly remarkable that, in trying to bring up children, a point is always reached (which may discourage or stimulate, depending on how one takes it) when the natural approach of the tactful parent doesn't work any more; and the strong will of the strong parent just as surely meets its waterloo. From this point on, nothing less will do the job than "unnatural" strength in the tactful one and tact in the strong one—a rise from natural habits of behavior to a level of higher authority.

Through marriage both men and women expect to find a helpmate who will support them in their weakness, praise them in their discouragement, and cheer them in their gloom. There is much of this in marriage, but there is also much of the opposite. Marriage, better than most relationships in life, teaches the paradox that the more help one needs, the less one will probably get. On the other hand, the less one needs, the more will be attracted. "For to those that have, to them shall be given; and those that have not, from them shall be taken away, even that which they have."

The same is true with discipline, as every parent and teacher has probably discovered. If one approaches a child while in a depleted state, one hopes for a certain sensitivity and restraint on the child's part—a moratorium on naughtiness. One is more likely to experience, however, a most unfeeling and immoderate outbreak of childish high jinks.

It may seem like very different matters to establish compatibility between adults in marriage and to establish educational discipline with one's offspring, but they have much in common; the requirements are identical. Whether one aims to achieve harmony with one's beloved marital antagonist, or wishes to help the children correct the faults passed on to them, life requires change.

"Love me, love my nature" is the ruin of marriage, just as "Obey me, obey my nature" ruins discipline. Adults do not love, nor do children wish to obey, what is merely native in another. As we become more "familiar" with what is only natural—in the sense what is typical and habitual—in another, our admiration becomes weaker.

Perhaps this is why the natural and lasting congeniality that newlyweds hope for soon becomes the opposite. Destiny has not joined them for the purpose of easy understanding and agreement but for instinctive polarity; it will ask them to learn the hard lesson of compatibility, which is achieved only through discipline and self-change. The goal for such a couple is to dearly love in one's partner what has overcome much for our sake.

This thought touches one's heart and will with such depth that effortless congeniality seems trivial. To have overcome a part of one's instinctual self for the sake of another calls forth, in response, love that contains the real experience of love—fresh surprise, beauty, and wonder. It also commands respect. This is especially true in our relationships with children. It is a gratifying dispensation for parents when they come to discern in their children a new feeling toward their discipline—a new feeling that arises, because they see the parents holding themselves to those same standards of discipline. They are also trying to respond to the inner voice that says: To be worthy of love, I must fundamentally change my ways."

The concept of discipline too often conjures up pictures of subjugation by a superior personality over an inferior one—of parents self-righteously and stubbornly insisting on the children's obedience. True discipline, however, is not a matter of the stronger bending or breaking the weaker; it is a mysterious interaction between two wills that are essentially equal in importance—even though, ideally, mature parents represent the higher kind of will that speaks for truth, warmth, and love.

In children, this higher aspect is still asleep. It must be lovingly awakened and stimulated to distinguish itself from the pushing and pulling of instinctive organic and environmental forces.

When parents customarily look up for divine guidance and heed what they receive, all will eventually go well, fundamentally, for the children. This is the mood and mode that they imitate. When parents consciously look upward to a divine source, the children sense divinity in their parents. Children are thus led in the right direction and gladly follow.

Thus parents must hold fast in trust and collaboration with the love and will that is higher than their own. If, at the time of discipline, parents think, feel, and act out of the same lower impulses that they deplore in their children—selfishness, pride, anger, and fear—there will be a battle of wills, both unworthy; their true spirit and will of the higher source will be powerless to awaken what is highest in their children.

True discipline awakens true discipleship, which is only an early stage of completely collaborative friendship; this is always the heart's glad choice. Obedience in childhood represents only the birth pangs of thoroughly independent freedom. These pangs are mixed with joy in the child's soul when the parents understand and hold their proper role.

In matters of discipline, children experience their mothers and fathers as reminders of the mysterious authority of the higher dimension from which our souls have descended to earthly life. Both parents stand for something that the children have retained as a kind of memory. But particular styles and approaches of mother and father are different. At her best, the mother represents sympathetic approval, helpfulness, and love. The father stands for a less sympathetic, more intellectual and commanding style, yet also loving. Ideally, both are firm, which derives from their trust in a greater wisdom and love, which they gladly serve as individuals. One may inspire loving kindness, encouragement, and patience. The other may inspire courage to claim independence and valor. Both are successful only through the respect they inspire, which depends on the overtone that should be heard through their own behavior—that is, their own attentive discipleship and devotion to the One. Parents' power to guide—without wearisome explanations, seductive bribes, or threats of violence—emanates primarily from their abiding sense of the Father/Mother above, for whom they know themselves to be representatives.

7.

PRESSURE AND
THE SPIRIT OF PLAY

Eternity is a child playing checkers;
the kingly power is a child's.—Heraclitus

WE LIVE TODAY under extraordinary pressures that exploit both humanity and nature. If modern civilization is to be renewed and positive again, there must be relief from these pressures. Relief must certainly begin with education. A man from another planet, observing conditions in an average school, could easily guess the state of the culture at large. Perhaps most notable about American students just now is the fact that their childhood is being shortened. Their teeth are changing earlier than they used to; they are maturing earlier sexually; they adopt grown-up modes of dress and behavior sooner; and they are playing serious baseball, football, basketball, and soccer before they reach their teens. It also seems generally true that the aptitude for abstract thinking is developing precociously among youth.

The curriculum of the modern school is partly following, partly causing, this trend to abandon childhood as soon as possible. Witness the demise of fairy tales and the introduction of reading—even of arithmetic and science—in kindergartens. Witness high school subjects shunted into the elementary school, and college subjects into high school. Consider the tactics of advanced placement and the movement toward lengthening the school year. Many of these impatient schemes betray the feeling that carefree youth, which would prefer to live for the sake of living, must hasten to leave toys and joys, and take up technical tools for a life that is Serious Business.

One symptom of modern education that is especially striking is the mania for swift reading. Children are encouraged, even harassed, to read faster and faster, as though academic progress were primarily a race with time, and speed of reading the very key to winning. In countless children and parents, the academic race inspires near panic.

The pressure of academic competition is deeply rooted in the orientation of Western culture. And it will probably increase despite the counter-trend of open classrooms, open curriculums, and the reduction of academic discipline in high schools and colleges. The kind of knowledge that is coveted increasingly compounds and subdivides, forcing itself upon the young. By accepting the challenge, psychologists are experimenting with techniques for awakening and stimulating pre-school children, even babies still in the crib.

The pressures of adult anxiety are shortening and restricting childhood. Pressures begin at the nursery level when parents, with an eye on college, insist that their children "learn" something. Children are asked to absorb more and more knowledge, and to absorb it faster, regardless of their normal appetites and aptitudes. They must appear to be thinkers long before experience has ripened any real thinking in them. Is it any wonder that the *knowledge* possessed by such children is so often joyless, and that their *thinking* is so relatively powerless, when, within the integrity of their own childhood experience, they themselves have had such a small part in developing either of these capacities?

This trend in our schools reflects the trends in adult society. The educational enterprise is turning into some great machine right before our fascinated eyes; standardized parts, assembly-line technique, time-and-motion studies, standardized quality control—all on behalf of mass production. We are even replacing teachers with machines. The presumed *hope* in all this is that mechanization will be as productive in education as it has been for industry. What are these pressures of mechanization doing for fundamental social well-being? The schools are turning out technicians who will in due course apply their remarkable skills to the creation of unremarkable values; but they are not building character, culture, health, or happiness.

We owe most of the power and the conveniences we all enjoy to mechanical techniques, or scientific industrialism. Although they seem to bring great blessing, comfort, and ease, we have not yet learned to control industrial technology and the galloping consumption of the natural resources upon which it depends, nor the cruel pace of life it sets for human and beast, nor the pollution with which it defiles the air, the water, and the Earth itself. We must soon discover and apply countermeasures, or we may look forward to a fearful and sick existence on a plundered, desolate planet.

It seems that, in our fascination with technological progress, we have almost lost the instinct for true progress. A sound economy will surely remember not to kill the goose that lays the golden eggs. Rather than undermine or deplete the natural conditions for human existence, it will seek to enhance them. An economy that respects natural conditions can spring only from the sound inner health of individuals themselves—out of their aesthetic sense of balance, their moral sense of justice, their practical sense of what works in the long run. A truly progressive economy, like the free, healthy spirit of all human existence, can function only to the extent that it can balance every one-sidedness with its opposite, bringing these opposite forces into a creative equilibrium.

Antidotes to Pressure

What forces do human beings need in order to oppose the pressures of a technological era? We must summon *counter-*technological forces to help us steer the proper course freely—just as we apply brakes to offset acceleration, or pull left on the wheel against a pull to the right to drive our car safely to a freely chosen destination.

To balance the techniques of *speed-up* for which education has prepared many generations in the West, coming genera-tions should be educated also in the techniques of *slow-down*. Looked at from one viewpoint, the rushing that exerts such pressure on modern lives comes from the fact that our civili-zation is overly addicted to the external side of existence. As our ends are largely materialistic, so are our means largely mechanical. But such material existence has not the power of renewal in itself. It is at the mercy of change, and the fate that rules all change on the purely physical plane is *entropy*, the law of progressive deterioration. We cannot catch up with this deterioration no matter how fast we run. If we want to stop scrambling and begin to walk like human beings, we must balance our present preoccupation with externality and its ever-changing demands through a strengthened awareness of the essential and changeless—that is, the basic realities that remain self-identical behind external change. To the extent that teachers can bring their students closer to essential, eternal being, to just this extent they will note that *time* is relaxing its grip upon them.

Ordinary science and technology fail to bring us closer to timeless Being. Timeless realities are indivisible and must be approached intuitively. Timeless Being eludes intellectual analysis, yet our present science relies almost exclusively upon the use of analytic methods. Other casualties of this fascination with dissecting, intellectual analysis is the possibility of experiencing the healing, unifying function of vital, living time itself—that is, as it evokes more diverse changes, it brings more clearly to manifestation the enduring, essential integrity and wholeness of particular being. The divisiveness of *clock*-time is now tending to gain complete ascendancy over the wholesomeness of *life*-time; and as human life becomes ever more tightly geared to the unfeeling pulsing of mechanical timepieces, we feel both fragmented and oppressed. We can find release only by learning when and how to stand clear of breathless mechanical time, so that the inherent creativity of real time may be appreciated as a kind of breathing.

External time somehow becomes meaningful and harmless when we find ways to dominate it from the viewpoint of timelessness. *Quality*, *essence*, and *being* are essentially timeless. Contemplation of the patiently generative aspect of *qualitative* time releases us from the remorseless, rushing aspects of *quantitative* time. As we surrender to such contemplation, the *present*, within which alone we can truly live—in which the "I am" experiences its reality—allows us to breathe freely. The future, which otherwise crowds the present, is forced to await our pleasure.

Students must learn how, as Emerson said, to live "in the present, above time," how to make time stand still by balancing the new-fashioned will to change things with old-fashioned gratitude and appreciation for the good in things as they already are. Such gratitude is awakened when the eye has been taught to discern *being* within *seeming*, essence within appearance, spiritual reality within physical existence.

Qualitative discernment can help us abandon our greedy plans to snare hypothetical future goods. Although Western tradition has taught us the virtues of purpose and planning, we must now realize that purposefulness serves human welfare only up to a point. It can surely be considered a virtue, yet at the same time it tends to increase the pace and pressure of life unless we also take care to cultivate its opposite in equal measure. If purpose teaches us to keep traveling, we must also learn how to arrive at last and to abide. Arrival and abiding might seem purposeless in that they have no goal beyond themselves. Travel usually seeks something that is elsewhere rather than here and now. Intrinsic values, on the other hand, are something within which one always feels at home. One lives and breathes in the present; love awakens as a consciousness of final goals attained. Learning to find values worthy of love—purely for themselves—is learning a secret rarely sought or practiced by modern methods of education, which tends rather to incite further the restless urge to keep moving.

Thus, besides learning how to go, children should be taught also how to stay. This requires finding a balance between external *pursuit*, which moves them toward distant destinations, and inward *devotion*, which actually draws those destinations closer. This inward appreciation expresses love, whereas the passion for outward activity manifests only desire. Students would thus absorb, along with prosaic teaching that encourages ambition, the more intimate logic of Emerson's observation: "What we love, that we *have;* but by desire we *rob* ourselves of the love."

Purposefulness implies postponed good. Today's children are already, even in the elementary school, too purposive. They need a heightened sense of the immediate *presence* and the availability of the values that really count. Purposefulness in terms of traveling toward distant material values in space and time must be replaced by loving devotion, which invites spiritual values into the immediate here and now.

One undesirable aspect of purposefulness is that it seeks to *use* life, too often dishonoring what it undertakes. Indeed, the exploitation of humankind, beast, plant, and Earth in our time follows the "cult of usefulness." Against such *instrumentalism* (modern schools reduce the sacred Word and divine *Arithmetica* to "tool" subjects), teachers must inaugurate a new devotion; we must help students cultivate the *useless*. Friends are useless, the flowers are useless. Art, poetry, drama, celebration, and worship are useless. Yet, the life that does not culminate in such qualities does not culminate at all. Every moment of life that ignores them is diminished and shortened, whereas any moment touched by such qualities is enlarged and prolonged.

Let us briefly examine the possibility of transforming the spiritless education that now undermines not only human vitality but the whole natural environment; for it is easy to imagine how a fundamental change in such education will bring blessings also for nature's world. Basic human needs will continue to mine the Earth of its metals and minerals—its irreplaceable substances. But is there not something we can do to at least balance this loss? What can we put in to replace what we are taking out?

We can give moral *value* in exchange for physical *substance*. We can return Good for goods. So we can seek to popularize, as it were, a new formula that expresses how matter can be transmuted not only downward to energy but upward to value. Through a more intimate, intuitive science, in material substances we can find the divine Ideas from which they came. Through a worthy artisanship, we can shape matter beautifully, creating a culture and a style of life that are truly works of art, worthy of the materials used. Thus, if at long last we *must* use up the Earth, we will at least have created blessed works that praise God, as do the lilies of the field. But, to do this, educators will have to give their students a decidedly different orientation. Presently, education focuses the tremendous energies of human consciousness upon Earth's precious substance, with the motive of serving, in more and more complicated ways, our appetites for food, shelter, clothing, and diversion.

We can imagine that a candle feels gladly sacrificed for the flame that serves intelligent activity; and firewood, for the flames that warm hearths and cheer hearts. The time has come for progressive, purposive Westerners to help youth's idealism and energy find creative, enduring ends that equally ennoble the sacrifice of Earth's substance.

The Power of Creative Play

Teachers must immunize students against every kind of exploitative pressure and awaken them to the ideal of a sound culture and economy on Earth. If we were to summarize the answers to the pressures mentioned (pressures levied upon teachers and parents and passed on to one another, to our children, and to the kingdoms of nature), such a summation might condense to a single maxim: *Play is the answer to pressure.* As life begins in play, so it should be carried on, and so should it end. The spirit of play is the only sound foundation—and cli-max—for a glad culture and a wholesome economy. Any teacher who feels the validity of this truth knows at least the direction healthy teaching should take.

We know that play characterizes childhood. Less often do we think of it as being also the very signature of maturity. Yet Christ was speaking of the mature person when he said, "Except ye become again as little children, ye shall not enter the kingdom of heaven." This might be paraphrased: Except in the spirit of play, human beings will not realize the divine in themselves, find the divine in the world, or participate wor-thily in the divine artwork of Creation.

Like the child at play, the mature person who has risen to childlike qualities is "in the world but not of the world"—close enough to shape things, yet free enough so that creative imagi-nation remains true to its own prompting. Nietzsche said that on our way to freedom we pass through three stages: the camel destined to be heavily laden with burdens and duties given by the outer world; the lion that fights courageously against pres-sures of whatever kind; and finally the childlike spirit, which in creative innocence, possesses freedom because it knows what it chooses to do.

Schiller, in his *Aesthetical Letters*, put the matter drastically but truly when he said, "A human being plays only when, in the full meaning of the word, such a person is human; and one is completely human only when playing." Schiller saw the "thinking" person as chained by logic, the "feeling" person as tossed by passion, the "working" person as compelled by fac-tual necessities. These functions must of course be exercised and these aspects of reality be acknowledged; but until the spirit of play finds its way into all of them, we are not free. The play impulse transforms the logical faculty into creative imagination. Play makes the work that deadens into art that enlivens. Play sets aside the storm and stress of passion for the quiet sense of freedom that fulfills itself as love.

Our work becomes play, therefore, to the extent that our own initiative completely cancels external pressures. Our love of the action itself makes light of the duty we feel to do it. The art of life therefore consists in transforming work into play. We should "play the game"—not in the sense of "playing along," but in the sense of knowing the rules, accepting them gladly, and then plunging freely into the sport for the joy it gives. Under these circumstances, we see that true play develops a more complete sense of responsibility than work, since in play we feel decisively "I choose and will," whereas in work we feel mostly "I am responding to compulsion."

The power of creative play mediates in perfect freedom between inner life and outer life. As the heart beats to inter-weave the nervous functions of the upper body and the meta-bolic functions of the lower body, the spirit of play actively holds forth between conceptual necessities in the life of thought and practical necessities in the life of action.

It is often assumed that play is occupied with unreality, and that coping with reality requires work. Our habit of thought assigns play to children and work to adults. Indeed, if grown men and women were permitted to regard life as a matter of play, we fear they would become irresponsible. The exact con-trary may be argued, however, because the ideal that play sus-tains is actually much more serious than most work. Play, as Schiller conceived it, is an exercise of caring and creativity, whereas in work much of the soul's depth may remain unen-listed. Play is a more complete undertaking than work, for play uses all our faculties, work only some. In play we lead our-selves; in work we are being pushed.

The energy for play is self-sustaining and self-renewing, but for work, the energy spent must be drawn from somewhere else. In this sense, play enriches life; work impoverishes it. Is it not clear, then, that the enjoyment, gratitude, and free activity that we have been calling *play* are closer to sound education, sound health, and sound economics than the unloved necessity and relentless, competitive pressure that goes by the name of *work*?

The Playful Tone for All Life

Nursery and kindergarten teachers should try to establish the fully active, fully creative spirit of play so firmly that it sets the tone for the rest of life. Then, in the early years of elementary school, letters and numbers—even literature, science, and history—should put down their first roots in the spirit of play. When presented imaginatively, they awaken free interest and lead to creative art through poetry and painting, dancing and singing, and play-acting.

This purely human, moral and aesthetic interest should be the goal of every school. Does not the very health of Western society ask us to remit the pressure of external purposes and selfish desires that now exploit us all, and even shackle nature unnaturally? Could not happier, more lasting contributions be made through the spirit of play? Society would undoubtedly prosper if ordinary men and women were educated to live their lives more creatively, with more fantasy and love; this is what happens when they are no longer so abstracted from earthly life as intellectuals, and not so deeply gripped by it as breadwinners.

The intuitive sense so closely connected with this spirit of play in youth makes it possible later on for the farmer to imagine more vividly how things look, for example, from the viewpoint of the apple trees themselves—or the cows, pigs, chickens, and earthworms. The farmer would realize for sure why she or he must move away from certain practices that the selfish, shortsighted, numb, dumb profit motive has introduced into agriculture. The same spirit of play that appears in such an imaginative identification with the creatures that the farmer masters and also serves, can be grace and salvation for all forms of natural life, including our own.

Imagine, for a moment, an injection of the spirit of play into business. What is closer to play than the making, trading, and transporting that make up what we call the economy? Are these activities and transactions only done to earn a living? They already *are* living. They spring from the mutual interplay of ability and interest. Wages are necessary, but vital individuals make the so-called work effort in any case; they are primarily concerned with the pleasure of being active at tasks. Vital men and women want humor, warmth, and vivid companionship with their co-workers. They love the sense of a significant function, however modest, in the scheme of things. They look forward to testing themselves against life and bringing forth their own initiatives to meet its challenges—for everyone's benefit. If the mainspring of all this adult *busy*ness were recognized for what it actually is—the instinct for play—the economic game would find ways to make itself more worthy of playing for its own sake and for the sake of wholesome, cordial fellowship on Earth; and wages would find their proper place in the scheme of things. When management no longer pursues personal profit as its main goal, labor will not feel obliged to fight so bitterly for the greater share it deserves.

If scientists would begin to pursue their research in Schiller's spirit of play, would not the methods and the findings of science change remarkably? Would not the patience of a more heartfelt wonder replace the merciless haste of mere curiosity? The will to capture the benefits of material power indirectly through intellectual knowing would be replaced by awareness of the forces of creative reality itself as it flows directly from nature into the human soul, whose knowing is more fundamental and complete. The perceived world, which has become empty material—because we are so hard-headed in our search for knowledge—would begin to relax and allow us to feel the immediate pulse of reality within appearances. Indeed, new powers of inquiry would arise with the ability to roll the stone of dead *fact* away from the grave in which materialistic preoccupation has laid the living spirit of *meaning*.

If scientists would recognize that true science is simply a form of play, they could lift their noses from the grindstone of analysis. They could look up and see, drawing together things both far and near, hidden and obvious, inner and outer. The proliferation of exclusively physical details—which is useful in many ways but always disappoints the soul's longing for wonder and blocks the heart's search for wisdom—would be absorbed by an increasing and deepening awareness of the living indivisibility of all *beings*.

The spirit of play can also bring light again into religion. In this spirit, men and women would feel closer to the all-fashioning Creator than they do when concepts of God are based on intellectual speculations about divine *judgment* and *purpose*. What is the "purpose" of trout in a mountain stream, of birds that give voice to the crystal air, of jungle tigers burning bright? Nature is a work of art; its forms are all divine fantasy. Is it not fruitless and false to imagine that pheasants and woodchucks, dandelions and geraniums (to say nothing of human beings to whom the Deity has given freedom of will) are the handiwork of a Deity motivated by no more than routine, practical "purpose?"

What is true of the religious feeling for nature may also be true of our human sense for destiny. Shakespeare echoes what we know of destiny from our dreams when he says that "all the world's a stage" whereon we humans have parts to play. Melville imagined the Fates as stage managers. Thus, one may venture that a dramatic imagination will often give a better clue to the roles we play in life than do legalistic ideas of punishment and reward. Fate may unfold according to aesthetic and moral necessities that are sensed better by the playwright than by the pedagogue or judge.

Regarding jurisprudence, one wonders whether justice could not be meted out to criminals more imaginatively or, as one might say, more playfully. We seem to ignore what no playwright or child at play would overlook—the actual relationships of life, the real issues between the criminal and the victim. A more playful judgment rendered simply out of the feeling for dramatic but loving justice could touch the heart of the wrongdoer in ways not possible for a more prosaic, censorious legality.

We must also consider the benefits to our culture when we properly value the innocence and joy of play in what we refer to as recreation and amusement. Through our general subordination of the play motif—though we give it so little value in other fields—we have arrived at a place where soul life is starved for both outlet and uplift. The concept of life we have been recommending to youth has become anemic and boring. Youth is therefore left to seek pleasure in coarse ways, through destructive physical stimuli. Yet it is really not bodily thrills that the soul desires—not a blow-out but release and updraft. Yet the present pursuit of recreation and amusement through exploitation of the body will not be halted by anything less fundamental than the multifaceted, multilevel spirit of play.

Health and the Sense of Play

Let us look at the heart. It is well known that diseases of the circulatory system—particularly the heart—are, in the West, the greatest single threat to health. This type of ailment, as a cause of death, is twice that of the next five diseases combined. Statistically, America has the distinction of being just about the most unhealthy country in the world. Mortality from this cause continues to increase and appears several years earlier in each successive generation.

What do pressures and play have to do with the heart? Among the causes of illness usually mentioned is the swift pace of modern life. We are told that it brings disorder into the circulatory system. This implies that we should live "less stressfully." On the other hand, we hear that the trouble also results from sedentary habits, and thus we feel stressed when we exercise. Or perhaps diet is to blame, and we should therefore try to eat less and eat better foods. Such worries, of course, are upsetting, and for peace we turn to tranquilizers. And, finally, since the tendency toward heart disease is said to be hereditary, those who hope to avoid it should select their grandparents with extreme care.

Research into the effects of stress on the human organism seems to indicate that, in a culture where freedom and fulfillment, love and joy, harmony and peace prosper, there will not be epidemics of heart attack. On the other hand, where initiative is cramped, where pressures crowd in, where enjoyment is superficial and where inner fulfillment is indefinitely postponed, men and women continue to find their overburdened hearts faltering.

Our American hearts are being squeezed both from above and from below. The drive toward intellectualism starts, in most elementary schools, with the kindergarten and it tightens and stiffens our children. And the ever-increasing mechanization of the whole environment contributes a further hardening influence. And, finally, hurry and competition (both based on fear) has adults trying to force their blood through a circulatory system already tightened.

It seems that, from the blood's point of view, we are living harder and enjoying it less. But blood really springs to its task, when the inner person feels free and, in that freedom, conceives an unmitigated *enthusiasm* for life. Blood flows through welcoming arteries when spirit opens human hearts to the world in love. Nothing less than this trusting, spirited love has power to cancel the fear that inevitably results from the lack of a spiritual orientation.

Education of the Playful Spirit

If reform is to become a renascence, it must begin in education. Many teachers would be glad to be the pioneers who replace fear-oriented materialism with the love-engendering spiritual awareness. But they need the support of society as a whole, especially parents. And many parents could not be in a better position to understand the need for a revolt against pressure, and to understand why the spirit of play represents much of what could lead such a revolt. They need only look around and into themselves.

We must realize, however, that pressure is not just an objective phenomenon, but is also subjective. It is not events alone—or even mainly—that press in on us, but we ourselves who *feel* oppressed, because of what is going on in our heads. At different moments of any day we are oppressed and then freed from oppression by circumstances that have not, of themselves, changed. Our mental attitude is what changes.

Considered as a mental attitude, what *is* stress? Pressure, worry, and stress are closely related. We can all see that our sense of pressure is basically a form of fear that arises when the world seems overbearing. Yet, ultimately, it is not the world that is too strong, but we who are too weak; and we are too weak in ourselves, because we are not fully *in* ourselves. Being overly aware of all that surrounds and besets us from outside, we become far too inactive in relation to our own center. Because of our time—our culture, our education—we are turned inside out, as it were. Fear is awareness (an "apprehension") of what comes from the outside and seems to close in and bear down. Only inner faith and assurance can give us the freedom necessary to play the real game of life. This trusting arises from within and flows outward from our hearts. This attitude alone answers the pressures levied by fear in its various forms.

Perhaps there cannot be too much awareness of the world, but there can be too little countervailing confidence and creative will in the self. This lamentable condition is the result of education that always calls on the nervous system without adequately stirring breath and blood. Such education develops a susceptibility to chronic fatigue and anxiety. Among many of our best students in our best colleges, anxiety and depression are increasingly frequent. Depression is a close relative to fear, a cowering of the inner person before the conditions and demands of outer life. Such depression can, at a certain stage, appear more organic than psychological, yet this may be an indication that the psychological effects of early miseducation are finally showing up in the physical body itself.

The spirit of play is the spirit of *freedom*. But we are free only when the opposing forces in our nature are held in balance. According to Rudolf Steiner, one primary force is cognitive wakefulness, whose instrument is the nervous system, centered in the head. The main opposing force is nascent will, whose instrument centers below in the metabolic and reproductive functions of the abdominal region. In heart and lungs, human freedom is born; they exercise the valiant rhythm that continually seeks to mediate between above and below—between what works inward upon us through the apprehensions of our senses, or nervous system, and what flows outward into the world through the will-force of our metabolism and limbs. Balanced, rhythmic interaction between these two systems cannot take place when negativity emanates from the upper pole and eclipses the positivity that waits to manifest from the lower.

The human self, one's I, experiences fear when feeling vulnerable. The I becomes vulnerable when it imagines being alone and adrift in an alien world, with which it has no fundamental relationship of mutual understanding and love. The self then thinks of itself as a subjective entity trying to find its way in a trackless objective world that essentially neither knows nor cares about one's personal needs and aspirations. The cold externality, the meaningless emptiness, of such a view of the world's structure and process is called *materialism.*

Materialism is the ultimate enemy of the spirit of play, which lives on the positive forces generated through faith, hope, and love. These, in turn, flourish only when the human soul feels at home in a world-order that is congenial and trustworthy—one that both knows *and* cares about the welfare of individual human souls. The self then expands and brings forth joyful zest and seeming abandon, because it is moved to contribute good from itself to meet the goodness it senses reigning everywhere behind and within the world of appearances.

A materialistic outlook hardens what should be the free outflowing of creative enthusiasm. Materialism reaches out through worldly ambition, but it is a form of self-seeking. It takes in but does not give. This orientation causes time to shrink and tighten. By contrast, faith's trust in the invisible, impalpable reality of spiritual goodness allows earthly time to relax by canceling ambition's vulnerability to fears of accidents, competition, and blind fate, all of which cause the breath of time to become breathless. By supporting hope, on the other hand, faith feeds time again and again with Eternity, causing it to become expansive, generous, and cooperative. When time fails to receive this higher nourishment, it is left enfeebled and abbreviated. Ultimately, life for materialistic players ceases to be fun.

Materialism breeds fear, and fear prolongs materialism. It congeals the joyful bounty of love's flowing, which becomes insatiable "wanting," selfish desire. The only forces strong enough to loosen and transform worry and anxiety are found in open-hearted admiration and gratitude. "Perfect love casts out fear," we are told. The enigmatic events, facts, and persons in the outer world become *lovable* only through what they represent inwardly—not outwardly and merely passing but lasting, not only of the body but of the soul and spirit (both of which antedate and survive the body). These transform desire back into love. They convert the precarious enterprise we call living here on Earth into the sacred adventure that is real life.

The dark prison of pressure is built by fear. We are opened and invited by love to freedom's joyful playing.

8.

THE QUALITY
OF LIFE ON EARTH

Q. Mr. Gardner, have you been following the reports about the abuse of our environment?[1]

A. I have read enough to be convinced that we are well into the greatest crisis humanity has ever faced.

Q. Were you already aware of the conditions now coming to light?

A. We learn something new every day, but the general picture has long been clear to those who love nature. This trend toward abusing the Earth has been evident for centuries. Thoreau saw it. Blake saw it. Maybe the Greeks foresaw that the Age of Iron would end this way. As long as only the Earth and the lower kingdoms of Earth were suffering, most people didn't care very much. But now the question is beginning to be one of life or death for humanity itself. This finally makes it seem serious.

---

1. Waldorf high school juniors were asked one spring, as a project in English and to increase their grasp of environmental problems, to interview concerned citizens in their communities. Some of the students interviewed me, and several of these interviews are summarized in this interchange; a few of the questions were from parents and teachers.

Q. Do you think there's any hope of solving the problem?

A. We must try, or see the Earth destroyed. Teachers probably have the most important job in this. They influence the next generation's thinking. That determines how they will feel and, in turn, how they act. Teachers are in a position to influence the beginnings of attitudes and behavior.

Q. What attitude, in your opinion, causes abuse of the environment?

A. I think our attitude toward nature starts, as do all attitudes, with certain ideas, or inadequate concepts. Modern souls have become estranged from nature. This means they are partly blind and partly don't care. Few of us are grateful to the world that sustains us; it rarely occurs to us that we should look to nature with thanks. This ingratitude has many causes. For example, the nature that most of us see is already sick; the freshness and beauty it has to give are under a pall. Then, too, our very concept of nature makes reverence or gratitude seem inappropriate. We have been taught the mechanics, dynamics, mathematics, and economics of natural processes, but we hear less and less of morality, spirituality, and divine life. How can we love a mechanical nature?

We have been taught that all beings are engaged in a competitive struggle for existence, each locked into kill-or-be-killed combat with others. Why should we be grateful to those who contest our very existence and want to do us in? We are also taught that our rationality, esthetic taste, and moral idealism operate within a universal context that is ignorant, indifferent, and, in the end, hostile toward natural creatures. We are shown human beings pitted against an all-powerful but basically inhumane world-process. Something that began with a "big bang" will have no scruples about a cataclysmic ending.

Many believe that as humans we are born accidentally, survive precariously for a brief moment, and then ignobly extinguished. If in this way we conceive of the natural process as our ultimate enemy, we can only feel put off, probably aggressive, and eventually cruel in dealing with nature?

Q. Do you think the modern scientific idea of the world is false?

A. In many details it is doubtless true; but the trouble is that scientists don't claim any longer to go beyond details. They leave it to others to formulate worldviews. But people need an idea of the whole; and when they look for the implications of technical data supplied by science, they come to the discouraging ideas I have mentioned. These ideas are very widespread; they are being given to children in the earliest grades of elementary school by well-meaning teachers throughout our land today.

Q. Do you see indications of any change?

A. It seems we are at the beginning of a profound change—otherwise, we would not be so suddenly aware of how estranged we are from nature and how hazardous our condition is.

Q. The recently growing interest in nature seems clear, but we wonder whether this perhaps is caused mostly by fear—of the consequences to ourselves—of what we have been doing wrong. How do you account for this new attitude?

A. The crisis of the environment has been in preparation for a very long time—hundreds of years, probably much more. The only thing new is the awakening. More and more people are beginning to see what has hitherto been systematically overlooked. Our consciousness has begun to change.

Q. What do you mean by a "change" of consciousness?

A. I mean a different way of thinking—one that concerns itself with intrinsically whole entities more than with collections of details. To see things this way requires intuition. It means learning to read words as well as spell letters. When you do this, the world changes. It begins to light up.

Q. So you think we have been living mostly in darkness?

A. Insofar as we are bright people, strong critical thinkers, and trained in scientific method, I believe we negotiate with the world from the outside. We are outsiders. When you are on the outside of anything, you are in the dark about it. Much of the technical knowledge about nature today is still being gained by methods that are called "experimental," but could better be called assault and battery. Life retreats and meaning conceals itself from this kind of approach. But life and meaning give light. The more we have learned about nature as matter and energy, the more we have lost touch with it as intelligence and beauty. In other words, progressive enlightenment of one kind has been deepening the darkness of another. But I hope we are beginning to—as Martin Buber said—*turn*.

Q. Can you apply this "turning" to the environmental crisis?

A. Any turning away from intellectualism toward intuitive understanding will lead to a renewal of warmth and conscience toward nature. If we can find again what people of long ago found in the natural environment—values that match what is intimate and basic in ourselves—we shall find ourselves at home again in the universe.

Q. But isn't it characteristic of the scientific view that human beings consider themselves very much as belonging to nature and being inhabitants of the universe?

A. So they do, but since most of us still regard nature materialistically, we tend to see ourselves in the same way. We ourselves are only facts among facts, organisms among organisms. But it is impossible for a human being to develop respect, much less deep affection, for mere objects. Therefore, though we fondly indulge our appetites, we do not basically respect ourselves. And this disappointment in ourselves, however unconscious, tends to become resentment toward nature. We feel no conscience about destroying it.

Q. You believe that a turn toward intuitive thinking can bring a whole new mood, so that people will again honor and love nature?

A. Yes. we do not exploit or degrade what we honor and love and take joy in.

Q. We think we follow you, but most of us are not quite sure we would know either *intellect* or *intuition* if we saw it. Can we get down to examples?

A. You don't lack examples of intellectualistic thinking. It is the basic tool of our day, in every walk of life. It is spelled out formally in the so-called scientific method: 1) Use physical senses to perceive physical facts. Use machines to extend or refine physical perception. Dissect and sub-dissect; lay everything open to perception. 2) Measure, count, weigh. Describe and name all parts, and parts of parts. Classify. Correlate. 3) Develop an abstract generalization. Formulate a logical hypothesis. 4) Test the hypothesis through repeatable physical experiments.

By using such procedures, we identify only material facts and establish so-called "laws" to explain them. Any attempt to go beyond dead matter to what actually inhabits, enlivens, and inspires matter can go no farther than making inferences.

Inferences lack substance. They hardly carry conviction and rarely kindle enthusiasm. If we are to know realities of the inner dimension, we need an inner form of perception as the basis for a higher kind of science.

Q. You seem to be saying that it is possible to perceive with higher senses. How are these acquired?

A. They appear as the transformation of ordinary thought, when love and patience have been added to it. Thinking that is concentrated and strengthened by love opens into a higher kind of perception. This begins as imagination. I believe that imaginative thinking, or spiritually-perceptive thinking, does not need to guess about life. It can participate consciously in living realities.

Q. What are we actually talking about? Suppose someone is looking at a rock, or a pool of water. Is an imaginative approach to these things open to an ordinary person?

A. Yes, even though neither of these things is directly alive. Both analytical and imaginative thinking would begin with the same physical observation of the water. But then the two paths diverge. Analysis would seek useful information by testing the water for weight, mineral content, boiling point, and so on. It would separate the water into the two parts of hydrogen and the one of oxygen.

Imaginative thought, on the other hand, would abide with the entity *water* just as it appears. The buoyancy, transparency, and fluidity of water would be allowed to impress themselves upon the observer and become matters of inner experience. Such outer-inner experience would no doubt be pale at first, but through repeated effort it would become strong. To experience the *quality* of water in the *substance* of water with complete objectivity is a good enough example of what I mean by real imagination.

Q. You believe, then, that ordinary people can become more at one with the things they see, and that when they do this, they can come to know these things from the inside—by penetrating them in this way, we find more than matter?

A. Yes. And this "more" is the only thing that can make us feel at home in the world or deeply interested in it.

Q. But I must ask again: how can we apply, in a practical way, what you call "imagination" to the present environmental crisis?

A. When we are educated to participate in the life of nature, we do not want to injure it; and we are not easily fooled about whether we *are* harming nature by seemingly clever actions of one kind or another. We will see things in context—alive and meaningful. From this sense of the living whole, we gain the instinct to distinguish between actions that favor health, beauty, and sanity, and those that are destructive. This instinctively sound judgment will then serve as the control for practical undertakings.

Q. Can you apply what you have said to some contemporary scientific or engineering problem?

A. Yes. Let's take a problem facing the Russian government: Should Russia try to irrigate parts of central Asia and replenish the dying Aral Sea by reversing the course of certain rivers that now flow north into the Arctic Ocean, thus making them flow southward? It seems that some scientists consider this feat technically possible. Or better yet, consider the proposal, on which our own government has already spent millions in preliminary studies: Should lakes be created by dams in Alaska where there is heavy rain and snowfall, with the accumulated water used to irrigate several western states, raise the level of the Great Lakes, and supply power as far south as Mexico?

I do not believe that technical science can answer such questions. Scientific method, as we know it, depends on experimentation, and there is no way to experiment with either of these vast projects. The wisdom required to foresee results without experiment goes beyond the ordinary human scope. My question is: Does humanity have any hope of accessing wisdom that is higher and more comprehensive than its own?

Q. Some kind of inspiration? Do you believe in that?

A. I must admit that I do. All the poets, saints, and seers who have cultivated imaginative forms of thought during the past millennia would agree that there *is* such a thing as inspiration, and that it does indeed bring practical wisdom. In former times, inspiration was for many not a belief but an experience. They asked, and they were perhaps answered by the very mountains and rivers, and by air and light themselves. It lies in the nature of imagination that its objects all tend to become subjects at last; its facts become beings. Every being has wisdom to reveal. That is what speaks in inspiration.

One hesitates to state one's true thought about such things, because people become either bewildered or angry when they hear it suggested that human religious traditions may not be entirely superstition. Such traditions tell us that divine will and wisdom are within and behind the external appearances of nature. Divine will and wisdom rule throughout all levels, living and dead, above and below. All beings have something to tell to those humble enough to ask and pure enough to hear. To some who have prayed, the inspiration may come as a new thought when they awake in the morning. In some it grows during the day as an obscure but persistent instinct for the right way. For seers it becomes a clear and conscious dialogue. But all who care and seek to see life as a whole, and who are not cut off by their own pride and cleverness, can find guidance that goes beyond human limitations.

Q. Aside from the possibility of higher guidance, we'd like to hear your own ideas about several of the difficulties now confronting us. For example, we could start with two developments. The first is the compounding increase in population; the second is our insatiable demand for goods that can be supplied only by plundering the Earth.

A. I do not believe in abstract extrapolations of the kind now being applied to the population problem. Mark Twain once observed that since the Mississippi River had shortened itself a mile or more every year by forcing a more direct channel through some of its bends, we could look forward in a thousand years or so to a Mississippi River only a mile long.

It is true, however, that we now have an overgrowth of population that is tending to overtax the natural environment. We do need to find a way to control this overgrowth. The only measures being proposed are contraceptive (and this must doubtless be worked on), but I am not persuaded that contraception goes to the root of the problem.

Q. If procreation is not the root of overpopulation, what is?

A. Since I have said other strange things, perhaps you will forgive one more. One has the impression that, although procreation obviously accounts for more babies being born, it does not account for any of the other forms of overgrowth that characterize our Western civilization. Consider, for example, the explosion of scientific knowledge—the drive toward mass production, extravagant consumption, monetary inflation, the faster pace of our whole way of life, and the phenomenon of megalopolis; above all, consider the prevalence of cancer as the disease of our time. Each of these examples of hypertrophy has its own explanation, yet they all have something in common, and I believe at some level they have a common cause.

Q. You think things in general today are getting too big and too many, and that what controls one can control all?

A. That may be overstating the case, but I am certainly interested in that line of thought. Hypertrophy seems to me to be an increase of *substance* unlimited by *form*; formless growth, anarchic growth, growth for its own sake, is the problem. The part should always remain subordinate to the whole. The growth of a single part is healthy and serves well only when it remains in proportion to the growth of all the other parts. Thus, we must look to the health and beauty of the whole if we wish to find the formative principle that should dominate growth of the parts.

Q. The analogy of other forms of overgrowth to that of cancer has been made before. But how does it help?

A. In cancer, as I understand it, the formative, proportion-keeping principle that should rule the whole of cell development is somehow broken down. In a certain area, therefore, the forces of growth run rampant. The part assumes for itself what should belong to the whole organism. As a result, tissues and organs are deprived, distorted, and eventually destroyed. I think of the overgrowth of cities, scientific knowledge, and our appetite for material goods as cancerous in this sense. In each case there is unbridled expansion of the part at the expense of the whole. This can happen only if the mysterious *ruling idea* that should dominate the whole has been weakened. I admit that I have hardly a clue about what the ruling idea might be that should control a phenomenon such as overpopulation. But I would try to find out by looking at matters macroscopically rather than microscopically. Too much analysis leads away from the answer.

Since we do not understand what we know, do not feel what we do, and develop powerful drives that threaten rationality, our soul and body are divorced from each another. I can thus imagine that our bodies would become anarchical.

Q. Are you suggesting that the body of someone who thinks feelingly, feels thinkingly, and acts through harmony of feeling and thought, will be different, and that cancer will therefore not develop in such an individual?

A. In medical questions I have only the layperson's right to use common sense. I am prepared to believe that when anyone is at one inwardly, such a person will tend to hold the metabolism and bodily form intact. Such individuals are hardy enough to resist anarchic breakthroughs. And I feel there must be an analogous relationship between what checks the overgrowth of cells and what (apart from contraception) prevents a population explosion. Maybe one of these days someone will be able to complete this notion, which I cannot.

Q. If you don't mind, I'd like to broaden our conversation about environmental crisis. This is, after all, a total problem, yet we've been speaking of solutions primarily from the viewpoint of education. Other social agencies should also be able to do something helpful. You have pointed out where you think education is making its big mistake, but do you have any ideas about what went wrong with agriculture, industry, or politics, that caused them to be unable to foresee and prevent what is happening to the Earth?

A. My competence lies in education. I am interested in other fields, but my ideas about them are quite general.

Q. I would be glad to hear of any change that you think business might make to improve the health of the environment, so that we could all look forward to a happier life than now seems likely for the future.

A. I have heard it said that there is as much suffering in the world as there is egoism. I also remember that the founder of Waldorf education, Rudolf Steiner, made this point long ago.

Self-interest is the source of the trouble between our economy and the world of nature. Self-interest permits us to ruin nature without noticing what we have done, much less feel sorry about it. Each individual looks out for his or her own interest, and feels quite righteous about doing so. The hired worker works for a living and the entrepreneur works for a profit. The accepted theory in America is that the profit motive has made capitalism great: Profit makes the wheels go round, produces wealth for all, brings about the affluent society, and so on. Yet, it seems obvious to me—despite Adam Smith's theory—that when each worker seeks, first and last, her or his own advantage, the economy as a whole will lack foresight and prudence. It will also lack the spirit of service. And before long it will tear the environment to pieces just as a school of minnows tears to shreds a piece of bread cast into the water.

Q. But if an activity becomes harmful, won't it eventually be stopped for selfish reasons—because profit falls off?

A. Not where nature is concerned—not until a resource has been exhausted or until a major catastrophe is imminent. The depletion of soil and food values due to chemicals, the multiplication of insect hordes due to monoculture in farming, and so on, have been well known for some time. Yet, such practices are not eliminated in agriculture, which is surely headed for disaster. When human beings are personally displeased by a product, they will eventually do without it, and thus change the producer's mind. They speak to some extent for themselves. But no one speaks for nature.

Q. You are suggesting that a farmer who cares less for profit and more for the soil, animals, and so on, would not exploit them. But won't the products be more expensive, at least in the short run, when a neighboring farmer can produce more, and do it more cheaply, by forcing?

A. That is why agriculture and animal husbandry cannot follow wise practices as long as the farmers who truly care for nature are at the mercy of those who aim primarily at short-term profit. The same thing applies to industry.

Q. You mean that the manufacturer who took adequate measures to protect the environment from pollution by a factory, and who did not want to sell more than people really needed, and who wanted to avoid waste by making the product last as long as possible, might soon be out of business?

A. Doesn't it seem likely? One altruist among many egoists in business may become a sheep among wolves.

Q. If that's the way things are. What do you propose? People *are* selfish; we can't start with a different human race or angels.

A. No. I contend that most people are actually no more selfish than they are unselfish. There is a world of sympathy and concern in most of us as we now are. The trouble is in our ideas, not in our feelings. There is a false *idea* that is widespread and tyrannizes our economy. This is the idea of profit as the ultimate motive of economic enterprise. This idea sanctions and promotes selfishness in economic life, even when people recognize in all other areas that unlimited selfishness is destructive. It keeps business people from following their natural inclination toward compassion and fellowship and their gift for teamwork. This form of the idea of profit should be set aside. Normal business people, as they actually are, could perfectly well replace self-seeking with a very different motivation—one more exciting, more satisfying, and far more appropriate to our current situation on this planet.

Q. What would such a motive be?

A. Service, friendly collaboration, and care for the future.

Q. I agree that, even as ordinary folks, we do care at times. We do take pleasure in serving some people sometimes, and perhaps what we call service activities are increasing. But can service really become the motive for economic endeavors? One could imagine such a change if our whole society were engaged with a goal that could inspire all of us, with leaders that inspire confidence. Then each person would perhaps feel the importance of doing his or her best for a common cause. But that is hardly true of our society. No one seems to comprehend where we are going, or why; so most of us go back to looking out for ourselves.

A. I don't object to looking out for oneself. But even self-protection will succeed only when we are genuinely interested in the rest of the world. Otherwise we will defeat ourselves no matter what we do. It is the essence of human nature to look beyond oneself. We are happiest when we are caught up in the pursuit of truth or adorning the world with a new creation or enjoying friends. Looking outward from ourselves, we are amused and inspired; we find work to do. It is the objective world that gives us our task; and if the world is pleased, we are pleased.

But I would like to return to your valid objection that one can hardly work for society as a whole when it has no common sense of purpose. We unite to some extent in a war, but in peace we fall into disunity. We look to peace as a time when everyone can prosper and find pleasure without interference, and such aims do not encourage a spirit of service.

It's not just because I am a teacher that I come back to education. If education gives no sense at all of the higher meaning of life on Earth, little inspiration to moral development, small desire to protect and enhance nature for its own sake, then we shall have no real common goals, and we shall not know how we may best serve society.

Q. Do you believe that if the schools can awaken imagination and inspiration, we can do these things and that business will get the right idea?

A. Precisely. I know we are far from where we should be, and it will take an immense force to rouse the nation out of egoism and materialism. But such an immense force is beginning to make itself felt.

Q. What do you have in mind?

A. I mean the sense of the catastrophe that will face humanity if we further despoil this planet. Substantial numbers of people are finally beginning to see that we cannot continue to make physical production and consumption the main goal of life. Earth can no longer stand it. The only goal other than material wealth must be goodness itself. Plato said that humanity's real goal is not goods but goodness. Goodness can be achieved only through the free choice and individual effort, and when the spirit of the whole awakens in each person.

Q. What you are proposing for economic life might sound like communism to many people.

A. Perhaps, but every "ism" has some kernel of worth. Although communism, in the Marxist sense, is thoroughly bad, communal purpose and effort are worthy aims. It was Saint Paul—not Karl Marx—who said, "You are many members, but one body."

Q. Are you saying that your idea of communal effort has nothing to do with political communism as state ownership of the means of production, the rule of economic processes by bureaucrats, and so on?

A. I am certainly not in favor of political communism, nor of the young people's communes, either, insofar as these involve drugs and sexual promiscuity. What I have in mind is an economy in which individuals are free to act out of their own expertise and initiative, in which they associate and collaborate by choice, and in which their economic *motive* is the public welfare.

One can sympathize with the social idealism that continues to draw naive people into the orbit of communism; but the idea of the state owning and running business is surely a bad one. State-run operations have always seemed either musty and mousy or unduly grandiose and extravagant. The state has no economic sense. It does not consider personal preference and smothers personal initiative. There is a proper sphere of activity for the state, but it has nothing to do with running the economy.

Q. We are glad you mentioned the question of government. What is your opinion on how the government has contributed to our present state. Many people say that only big government can now force the economy into line by passing stringent new laws and releasing vast sums of money to reclaim the air and water. Even some conservatives appear to be asking the government to intervene in business.

A. I know even less about politics than about business. There is, however, a certain advantage in ignorance. It greatly simplifies questions. I have a single strong conviction about what government has done wrong and what it could do right in regard to our treatment of natural resources and the Earth's environment in general. Men and women should be able—simply as human beings—to express their preferences in certain matters and make them stick. If people want their children to have a healthy environment in the future, they should be able to demand it. After stating their will in the matter, it should be binding on all economic activities that affect the environment. This should set the absolute limit within which these activities operate.

Q. You believe that government exists to bring about such consensus and give force to it. By passing laws?

A. Yes, by passing and enforcing laws.

Q. Is there anything new in your idea? Don't we pass the laws we think necessary?

A. We pass many more laws than we enforce, unfortunately. And a massively broken law seems worse than no law at all.

But, do we pass the laws that we as human beings really want? I doubt it. The issues that come up for vote are often so remote from our experience or so complicated that most of us can hardly remember being asked the kind of direct question that we would feel competent to judge with common sense and from the heart. Why were the voters not asked, long ago, to state unequivocally their desires regarding fresh air, clean water, and so on?

Q. Do you think people really want a wholesome Earth more than they want nylon stockings, plastics, cars, and airplanes? Would they vote for a sound environment if it meant giving up these things?

A. I don't know. I admit that Americans have willingly closed their eyes to the cost of many processes in industry, mining, forestry, and agriculture. Because of lack of education people are insensitive to any higher nature and, as a result, do not feel strongly about the ugliness and cruelty of what technology is doing. Still, we are not altogether dead to these concerns, and we are certainly alive to the issue of our survival and that of our children. We could have faced certain issues long since.

Q. Why didn't we?

A. Partly, I think, because there are powerful economic lobbies in politics, where they don't belong. These interests would find it inconvenient for voters to decide in purely human terms— spiritually envisioned and understood—how the Earth's environment may be used.

Q. But isn't that what democracy is: the interplay of various interests?

A. I think not. There must be economic pressures, but their adjustment should take place not through politics but within the economic life itself. If business people—consumers, distributors, and producers—would get together, economic questions could be judged by those who have experience, and managed by those who have the ability, as long as the overall purpose truly serves, in the highest sense, the common welfare.

I am advocating a few simple but comprehensive standards of decency and common sense that could be established by an electorate voting as genuine equals. Don't forget that the essence of democracy depends on people voting *as equals*. Individuals are not the equals of pressure groups.

It is also foolish for people to vote on questions to which they are not equal. The kinds of questions on which one person's feeling *is* as good as another's are bound to be elementary, nonspecialized, and simply human. They are not economic or scientific questions, but matters of fair play, conscience, and intuitive consensus.

For example: Do we have the right to enjoy freedom of thought and choice regarding our primary values in philosophy, science, art, religion, and education? Should all children have the same educational opportunity regardless of their parents' bank account? Should we forbid the economic exploitation of human labor? Should we guarantee support of the aged, infirm, and indigent? Should we protect ourselves against violence and criminal behavior?

If economic interests were not diverting and confusing the electorate, and if these same interests did not have the power to block legislative and police action, people today might be ready to come to a resolution something like this: We want laws that further limit the kinds of production and consumption that are ruining the Earth's environment.

I would also hope for a positive resolution to match the negative—a national policy that gives citizens, especially when they are young, the chance to work actively at restoring and enhancing the health and beauty of nature.

Q. Do you realize how unconcerned most people still are? But who knows just how much production and consumption will ruin the Earth? And, who can restrain or transform technology as long as people are used to material wealth and view machines as work savers? Keep in mind that there will be millions more people every year making such demands.

A. You are right, but so am I. Regardless of improbabilities, even impossibilities, that derive from bad habits, bad education, and trends beyond our control, the chance must exist for citizens to establish ideals and standards on matters in which the only interests are purely human interests in the best sense. At present, economic interests play forcefully into the legislative process, and it seems that government must purge itself of these interests.

Q. You want the government out of business entirely?

A. Yes. When a government tries to manage the economy, it must expect economic forces to manage it eventually, and this is happening everywhere. The true business of limited government is to safeguard simple standards for our community life.

There is yet another area that I think the state should retire from—and this is the most important change I suggest. Since it touches what I know best, I propose it very strongly. This involves the so-called public school system.

Q. What would be the advantage of such a move?

A. I have tried before to state some of the advantages[2] and to answer a few of the questions that arise whenever one suggests disestablishing the public school system and replacing it entirely with independent schools. The point I'd like to make now, however, is specific to the environment and to our initial discussion.

Q. We started with your idea that we abuse the Earth because we don't love it. And we don't love it because we view it as strangers. What we need is to be educated in intuition leading to love. Is that right?

A. That is the very point I want to emphasize. There are many reasons for the fading of imagination, inspiration, and intuition in our time. Padraic Colum says that the imagination used to be exercised during the evening in every home through story-telling.[3] The advent of electric lights ended that. Many changes must now occur in education if real imagination is to come alive again; but the step that could make all the difference is to grant full independence to education.

Q. It's hard to see how freeing schools from state control would help to develop intuitive knowledge. Why wouldn't it have the opposite effect or other effects?

A. In individual cases, an independent school may ignore or

2. "Toward a Truly Public Education," *Proceedings* No. 18 of the Myrin Institute, Inc., 1966; and "Independence for Education," in the October, 1967, issue of the National Association for Independent Schools *Bulletin*.
3. Padric Colum, 1881–1972, typifies the best of the Irish literary renaissance of the early twentieth century. Author of many children's books, among them the classic, *The King of Ireland's Son*, Floris Books, Edinburgh, 1986.

even stultify the intuitive side of its children. But it is more likely that the very fact of freedom in education would, for the most part, move schools toward qualitative, spiritual values, which state control currently considers out of bounds.

Just imagine: What would happen if *all* students and their parents were in a position to look for a school purely for the values it represents? Personal *interest* would become real *involvement*. Such involvement would lead to enthusiasm and initiative among parents as well as among the students. Now, picture teachers who are freed from externally imposed objectives and standards. They face each student with only two goals: first, to find the particular good strength in each student, and second, to draw it out. The teachers' task is to bring their own best and deepest to meet what is best and deepest in the student. Under these conditions, education develops according to intrinsic rather than extrinsic motivations. Curriculum and method come alive. Not only is the subject matter more imaginatively and intuitively taught, but the students become far more creative and satisfied.

Freedom stirs the will. The will is the creative part of human beings. When thinking is felt and thoroughly willed, it no longer plays upon the surface of things, but penetrates. The surface of the world is matter; the depth is spirit. When thinking becomes active, because it is free to pursue and care for what counts most, it gains strength to pass beyond matter to what enlivens it. Activated thinking finds the creative spirit in, behind, and above all things. If this spirit is freed to come alive in schools, we will enter a new era. Our relationship to nature will change radically, and wisdom will replace cruelty in the ways we treat the environment.

Q. You seem to have great hope for freeing education.

A. I do, indeed. When teachers can settle down quietly to the real business of education—which is to awaken, empower, and improve human beings—they will be happy in their work. When children are taught in this way, they respond. Compulsory state schools are free to emphasize only external goals and pressures. But independent schools can emphasize the primary values in life, which enable teachers and students to hear what life has to say to the heart and conscience. And this will bring about what we need more than anything: an end to the ravaging of our wonderful planet.

At present we expect nature to serve our purposes, and we bend it to our pleasure. Yet we feel no lasting pleasure, and we have no real purpose. Thus, what we have justifiably mastered becomes unjustifiably exploited. Our emptiness craves to be filled. Joy would fill it. Meaning would fill it. Grateful love would fill it. But the ordinary, external way of looking at things does not allow joy, meaning, reverence, or even gratitude. Because of our empty souls, ignorant greed for material goods and services becomes insatiable. As long as this displaced craving rules in us, no laws will succeed in curbing our suicidal mania for consumption. Continuing in this way will destroy this unbelievably lovely Earth, which should be the source of humanity's greatest hope for the future.

9.

THE POVERTY
OF A RICH SOCIETY

We call the holding in the hand, or the house, or the pocket, or the power, having: but things so held cannot really be had; having is but an illusion in regard to things. It is only what we can be with that we really possess—that is, what is of our kind, from God to the lowest animal partaking of humanity. —George Macdonald

In any kind of society, the healthiest, happiest and most creative persons are likely to be found among those who consume least.... In the United States, the average consumption of energy per person today is approximately double what it was thirty years ago and double also what it is now in Europe. Does anyone really believe that this difference is reflected in more happiness, less suffering, greater longevity among present-day Americans, or in a more rapid progress of American civilization toward more desirable goals? —René Dubos

GROWING WORLDWIDE POVERTY—the plight of those without life's barest necessities—is cause for compassion and concern in many who have more than they need. The more prosperous nations occasionally extend gestures of help, prompted in some cases by the guilt that affluence feels when confronted by want. Perhaps there is also a feeling, in some obscure way, of responsibility. Even less obvious, perhaps, are the first twinges of fear.

Those subtle feelings of responsibility, guilt, and fear among the prosperous toward the poor, however, are not allowed to get out of hand, and are largely ignored, even denied, in favor of practicality and common sense. After all, what can *we* do beyond offering some prudent measure of our own wealth and some sound advice as to how others may utilize the economic practices that have made us so wealthy?

The purpose here is not to explore direct, cause-and-effect relationships between the economics of "developed" versus the poverty of "undeveloped" nations—although such relationships certainly exist. The purpose is to examine the facts and techniques of wealth here in America—the land that has long led the world in the production and distribution of commodities—and to see clearly what lies before us in the American culture.

Has American "know-how" really conquered poverty? Is the advice we have to give poorer peoples as sound and good as we claim? Is it possible that American society, which has come to represent conspicuous consumption, is *also* conspicuously impoverished?

Poverty is the general term for what we are beginning to see everywhere in this wealthiest of nations. This poverty, which is still primarily an inner condition, is rapidly coming to expression in external ways that affect everything from the health of human beings and animals to the value of the dollar, from the actual worth of our commodities to the quality of our whole environment.

When we study the faces of men and women walking the streets, thronging the stores, or serving the needs of a city, we too often sense a hidden vacuum, a kind of gasping of the soul for what should be an atmosphere of normal fulfillment. Even the faces of school children frequently tell a similar story: stolidity and indifference have settled on so many of them, as though animation were partly suspended for lack of some all-important ingredient in their experience of home and school.

We know that millions of Americans in both rural and urban areas are ill-fed, ill-housed and ill-clothed. Yet how many gleaming, cheerful, well-centered faces one sees among men and women whose livelihood is meager; and how many clouded, petulant, craving faces among those who seem to have everything. Who is poorer? If want cries out so painfully, so balefully from the squalor of ghettos, how much of *that* sense of want is precisely the need for more adequate food, housing and clothes, and how much results from the *inner* deprivation and disappointment so much like that of the pampered rich?

Hunger of the Soul

Without distinguishing between those with money and those without, we can say that most Americans today suffer from a hunger of the soul, which they try to satisfy through overeating, smoking and drinking too much, spending more than they have, addiction to TV, and simply going too fast. Unfulfilled hunger drives them to self-destructive life-habits, and the growing gap between what they *need* from life and what they are *getting* opens them to anguish and despair, which they try to suppress with sedatives, stimulants, and mind-altering drugs in enormous amounts and at enormous cost.

Materialism robs American souls of security, hope, and enduring forms of enjoyment. Materialism devours, just as sensuality does. But the hollowing of human hearts by mechanistic thinking and the atrophy of human wills by over-dependence on machines can be concealed as long as material abundance prevails. Men and women in shopping centers may not believe that they are hungry for more than what presents itself on the store shelves. People who can buy bigger, faster cars every couple of years may scoff at the idea that those cars may actually lead away from satisfying more fundamental desires. While it lasts, material opulence certainly has power to delude us into thinking dark is light, down is up, ugly is beautiful, and bankruptcy of soul is fulfillment. But when materialism fails to deliver even its own kind of goods, *then* we hear an outcry.

We are entering an era of material discomfort and shortage that stretches far into the future. Long-standing deficiencies in the taste and nutritional values of our food have been pretty well ignored. We all become serious, however, when diminishing fertility of the soil, sinking water tables, rapid exhaustion of seed stocks, unfavorable weather patterns, and so on combine to threaten even the quantity of the foods to which we have become accustomed.

We are presently witnessing everywhere the failure of materialism. This would be an encouraging sign if old thought-habits allowed us to perceive this and adopt new perspectives. Few have any real sense of the plight of Western industrial society. There are too few proposals for reform that can dig to the roots of what ails us. Far too many people still believe that the symptoms of deficiency in our souls, environment, and energy supply will be short-lived and will be cured by larger doses of the poison that is bringing us down in the first place—that is, through the magic of technology.

Western civilization is now in the process of being judged by the ideal it has chosen as its own—that of material wealth and comfort. As though sounding the only trumpet loud enough to awake us, chronic shortages in the *quality* of life are becoming acute shortages of *quantity*: building materials, metals, electricity, gasoline, heating oil, fertilizers, water. The rapidly growing world population is making its demands just in this time of incipient shortages. The poor of all nations (inspired by the well-advertised desires of the affluent to consume more) are beginning to add to the mounting pressure on ever-diminishing resources.

Essential to an affluent society itself, of course, is money. The world-wide inclination toward inflation means that money is being progressively impoverished. It buys less of what is available. On the heels of inflation follow economic depressions, which mean that less is available at any price.

The world is drawing together as one. Therefore, the poor suffer poverty and the rich their equally real though different impoverishment, and an intense interaction is beginning to take place between them. Poor nations must assume the impoverished perspective and attitudes forced upon them, wittingly or unwittingly, by the rich, thus adding poverty of soul to poverty of body. The rich nations, however, will come to share the purely physical want, which the poor, in turn, will eventually force them to face, either through moral persuasion or blackmail. Whether or not the rich nations would like to remain oblivious to the poor—wherever they may be—they will not allow it. The poor have been not only awakened to the idea of human rights and the possibilities of legitimate political action but have been inoculated with the craving for material affluence and alerted to the possibilities of achieving political and economic ends by terrorism, oil and drug cartels, atomic threat, and so on. Poverty unwillingly borne—as it always is in a materialistic culture—awakens a primitive predatory egoism. The conflict of all-against-all could have only such a beginning: a full arousal of limitless hungers in humanity along with a gradual diminishing of the means to satisfy them.

Poverty is likely to become the scourge of the future; it is behind many forms of suffering and strife in the world today. In spite of the apparent affluence of a few nations—even because of it—in this age of pressure and craving, humankind as a whole is poor and becoming poorer. Whereas there are many who are poor both outwardly and inwardly, those who are the richest outwardly are among the poorest inwardly.

In his book *The Failure of Technology*, Friedrich Georg Juenger asks: Does scientific technology, mechanization, and industrialism—the proud achievements of the West—really lead to an abundant society? Do these ways of handling life create riches or destroy them? Juenger says that it depends on what we call "riches." There are, he says, riches of being and riches of having. The latter are not the true gold, for they do not bring security, happiness, peace, personal power, or even the lasting assurance of plenty.[1]

Juenger argues that industrialism, far from being productive, is exploitative; for its machines always consume more than they produce. His argument is borne out by the experience of American agriculture, which is generally thought to be the very example of abundance as produced by applied science, and yet which expends, according to recent calculations, as much as twenty units of energy (almost all of it being energy drawn from irreplaceable fuels) to bring one unit of food-energy to the consumer's table. Juenger says that experts come to this conclusion by exact bookkeeping, but that we can be convinced of the same general truth by simply observing what is all around us. We need only look to see that machines, when in action, devour; and when inactive, appear hungry. Centers

---

1. Friedrich Georg Juenger, *The Failure of Technology*, Henry Regnery Company, Chicago, 1949.

of industrialization have a concentrated forlorn—if not a destructive, rapacious—quality. They are the very picture of a greedy will to consume that impoverishes the Earth.

Juenger, writing over forty years ago, did not deny the advantages of machinery, but intended only to dispel illusions that prevent humankind from comprehending why all is not well in the modern world; why everywhere we see signs of impoverishment. He wished only to make clear that the great advantages of industrialism, which permit some to have so much, are bought at an undeniable cost to those same human beings, and indeed to the whole Earth. In order to measure true abundance, Juenger asked his readers to look at a country landscape where all is green and growing, budding and fruiting, and producing what was not there before—yet in peace, health, and beauty. In field and forest we find neither devastation nor waste as the by-products of growth. The natural landscape, when tended with love and wisdom, enriches itself ever more, for the benefit of all who live in it. It gives us the picture of a true economy and a real productivity.

The alchemy of life makes increase; the alchemy of death makes decrease. The former is a spring rising within itself to flow beyond itself. The latter is a vortex that draws inward from all sides, sucks down, and disappears within itself. The flowing spring shows how being renews itself and spreads blessing so that all are enriched; the sucking whirlpool shows how the craving to *have* lures existence into the abyss of non-being.

Juenger attempts to show that the world, as it is currently directed, will experience ever-increasing shortages, and that these will result from our dependence upon industrial mechanization. He reasons, however, that industrialism is simply applied science, and that behind our technical science lies a certain way of thinking. This mode of thinking is the final culprit. *This* is the sucking whirlpool, the negative spring. The abstract intellectuality underlying science today is turning Earth's living reality into a "photographic negative" of itself.

This power of abstraction that characterizes the modern mind is undoubtedly a significant achievement. The ability to lift oneself deliberately out of merely instinctive, sensory and mental experience through focusing attention with faith and love on a purely conceptual content is surely an advance for human thinking. It is a step toward clear, free, spiritual perception in a fully modern sense. To reach this goal, however, takes more than one step in the right direction. We cannot really pass beyond the physical if, at the last moment, we cling to it out of fear.

If, instead of allowing the modern capacity for pure thought to kindle into spiritual life, we get caught in the limbo of mental abstractions serving physical appetites, we abort the evolution that should occur in our own development; at the same time we cast a blight over both our natural and social environment. Instead of reaching through physical and intellectual reality to lay hold of its source, the abstracting mind stops short at the less than real. One result is the machine civilization, as well as the current fascination with "virtual reality." As this abstract intelligence spreads its net more comprehensively, and as it delves more ruthlessly into natural existence, it will convert inner and outer life more swiftly into plastic facsimiles of itself.

By following Juenger's analysis, we begin to see how poverty is intimately related to humanity's present experience of knowledge. This realization is a very hopeful turning-point, for if the impoverished experience of knowledge eventually makes us all poor, we have every reason to expect that an enriched experience of knowledge will bring us wealth of soul, and even of body.

The Sources of Poverty

Before returning to this positive prospect—indeed, the *necessity*—for humanity's renewed health, we must first review how we arrived where we are. Two philosophers have best represented the main trend in the American way of life: John Dewey and William James. Dewey, whose influence dominated American education during the early twentieth century, devoted his life to justifying and glorifying modern natural scientific methods. In his essay "Nature, Means and Knowledge" he characterized natural scientific thinking. "Intellectual meaning," he says, is always "instrumental":

> In responding to things not in their immediate qualities but for the sake of ulterior results, immediate qualities are dimmed, while those features, which are signs, indices of something else, are distinguished.[2]

To look beyond the "immediate" qualities of a thing, element, or creature, according to Dewey, is to search out its essential character at a deeper level than superficial appearance. One cannot quarrel with such a method. But what if the search for the kind of meaning that the technical sciences consider most usable leads us to prefer the abstract and mechanical to the vital and real? H_2O, Dewey suggests, is more "useful" to us than water. In a certain technical sense he is of course right. But water—as mist and rainbow, as healing balm, as quencher of physical and spiritual thirsts, as the very symbol and promise of abundant life—has meanings for human beings that go far beyond H_2O. These meanings may

---

2. *Experience and Nature*, The Open Court Publishing Company, LaSalle, Illinois, 1929, pp.107-108.

contain medical and agricultural wisdom overlooked by H_2O science. Beyond the art of living, joy and strength for living can be learned from an imaginative, intuitive study of water in its immediacy. Those who hope to reap future technical abundance and overlook present living abundance may find at some point that they have outsmarted themselves, trading their inheritance for a mess of pottage.

Another thing of note in the brief statement by Dewey concerns scientific method as what always works from "ulterior" motives, or the real aim behind actions and stated motives. Dewey was a good Yankee; he was strong on the *use* of things in God's world. That is why he was pleased to call his philosophy of science *instrumentalism*. But we don't trust anyone who wants to "use" us. We know that no good will come of it. And this naturally leads to a question concerning "scientific" dealings with nature, in Dewey's sense: Can lasting good—that is, real and lasting abundance—come from a method of cognition whose will to power over nature exceeds its respect and love for nature's living integrity?

> In principle, the step into such a technical science of nature is taken whenever objects are so reduced from their status of complete objects as to be treated as signs or indications of other objects.[3]

One is reminded of a politician who courts people as potential voters, or of a lawyer who handles a case not to defend a just cause, but because its unjust cause may prove profitable. One thinks of someone who looks past the personal integrity of another human being and sees a "love object".

---

3. Ibid, p. 109.

Enter upon this road and the time is sure to come when the appropriate object-of-knowledge is stripped of all that is immediate and qualitative, of all that is final, self-sufficient.[4]

That is one way to express the difference between the *way of knowing* that chooses to remain with the fullness of reality intact and one that, for technical advantage, strips the natural world of everything that makes it beautiful, dear, and alive. It is the difference between the complete, creative experience of love and the incomplete, impure, and destructive experience of lust.

Yet Dewey says:

Genuine science is impossible as long as the object esteemed for its own intrinsic qualities is taken as the object of knowledge. [5]

Can one believe that a genuine science would concern itself with anything other than precisely intrinsic qualities? But just this inadequate way of thinking has been with us for a long time. We are told that it accounts for all our great material progress. Dewey quotes William James, his predecessor in pragmatism:

Take those aspects of phenomena which interest you as a human being most ... and barren are all your results. Call the things of nature as much as you like by sentimental moral and esthetic names, no natural consequences follow from the naming.... But when you give things mathematical and mechanical names and call them so many solids

---

4. Ibid.
5. Ibid.

in just such positions, and describing just such paths with just such [6]velocities, all is changed.... Your "things" realize the consequences of the names by which you classed them.

William James was far from Henry David Thoreau, who appealed to warm-blooded intuition rather than cold-blooded intellect to understand nature more deeply. Thoreau stated his view by saying that one "who would understand nature must practice more humanity than others." Not *less* but *more* of the esthetic, moral and religious response basic to being human is needed for true insight into Nature. Would not Thoreau have asked whether the pure redness of the rose—far from serving us as a sentimental diversion—is really the essence of the rose? If science impoverishes beings by ignoring their real presence, does it have the capacity to guide human civilization to genuine health and abundance? It is more likely that, as James said, "your 'things' realize the consequences of the names by which you classed them." The pragmatic outcome of a science that makes a "photographic negative" of the world will eventually be a world as cold and empty as a photographic negative.

The practical results of modern science may be seen in practice. For thousands of years farmers knew how to irrigate their fields without ruining them as is done now through inadvertent salinization; and those same farmers—basing their approach to the land squarely upon esthetic and moral intuitions—maintained the fertility of their soils indefinitely. Modern agriculture, on the other hand, induces only a semblance of fertility by injecting nitrogen, which in twenty years

---

6. Ibid., pp.109–110.

may have to be intensified fivefold to produce the same amount of crops.

Dewey continues:

> To know, means that men have become willing to turn away from precious possessions, willing to drop what they own, however precious, in behalf of a grasp of objects which they do not as yet own.... The great historic obstacle to science was unwillingness to make the surrender, lest moral, esthetic and religious objects suffer.[7]

These are plain words, and they bear directly on the subject of soul poverty in a rich society. To *know*, says Dewey, first requires a vow of esthetic, moral, and religious poverty—that is, turning the soul's inner life into a desert. Or, to speak more pungently, it requires that one cleave to ugliness, evil, and meaninglessness, forsaking all concern for beauty, goodness, deeper kinship, and real intelligibility.

Dewey says that to know is to turn *away* from precious possessions that carry within themselves the intrinsic power to satisfy and enrich the soul and to conceive a craving for what one does not have and will not satisfy when obtained. Can one imagine more exact instructions for building a society that runs faster and faster to no end, fruitlessly exhausting itself and the resources of its planet?

We must be grateful for the early efforts of those such as William James and John Dewey, who lay bare the mode of thinking that has made possible all the techniques of materialism. The prospect of abundance or poverty in the years ahead

---

7. Ibid., p. 110.

depends on whether we continue to place our hopes in the further development of this same thinking. We are today in a better position to appreciate the full force of Juenger's argument—that is, as technology becomes increasingly unrestrained and ubiquitous, humankind and nature alike will be broken on the wheel of poverty.

> Progress in its present rapid advance creates an optical illusion, deceiving the observer into seeing things which are not there. Technology can be expected to solve all problems which can be mastered by technical means, but we must expect nothing from it which lies beyond technical possibilities. Since even the smallest mechanical process consumes more energy than it produces, how could the sum of all these processes create abundance? There can be no talk of riches produced by technology. What really happens is rather a steady, forever growing consumption. It is a ruthless destruction, the like of which the Earth has never before seen. A more and more ruthless destruction of resources is the characteristic of our technology.[8]

---

8. Juenger, op. cit., p.22. A many-sided treatment of this issue appears in E. F. Schumacher's *Small is Beautiful*, Harper & Row, New York, 1973. Mr. Schumacher is clear that much of what we call production is actually consumption: "I started by saying that one of the most fateful errors of our age is the belief that the problem of production has been solved. This illusion, I suggested, is mainly due to our inability to recognize that the modern industrial system, with all its intellectual sophistication, consumes the very basis on which it has been erected. To use the language of the economist, it *lives on irreplaceable capital which it cheerfully treats as income*. I specified three categories of such capital: *fossil fuels*, the *tolerance margins of nature*, and the *human substance*." (p.19)

If genuine economics is the art of creating and maintaining an "order of plenty" based on what nature provides, then technology, if unchecked in its motivating forces and methods, is at present anti-economics. It presupposes destruction because it works by destruction.

> The radical consumption of [irreplaceable] oil, coal and ore cannot be called economy, however rational the methods of drilling and mining. Underlying the strict rationality of technical working methods, we find a way of thinking which cares nothing for the preservation and saving of substance.[9]

Is not the "care nothing" attitude noted by Juenger reminiscent of James's and Dewey's recommendation to divest nature of everything qualitative and intrinsically precious? It is only a short step from the technical mind that strips quality from everything it touches to the technology of strip-mining the Earth for ores, coal, and oil.

"To those that have shall be given"

Two wrongs do not make a right. America has redoubled its technological efforts at energy self-sufficiency through offshore oil wells, exploiting Alaska, strip-mining coal, building atomic power plants, and so on. Although many of these projects may be justifiable in the short term, they cannot eliminate the problem of the poverty now looming over this affluent nation's sense of optimism. We must instead begin to replace quantitative technological thinking with an attitude that restores the *living* and the *qualitative* to our hearts. That

---

9. Ibid., p. 23.

is the only way to true economy, and the only way to pass from worry, want, and toil to creative well-being and happiness. In order to achieve economic renewal and alleviate our inner hunger, we must learn from Saint Francis' "Song of Brother Sun."

To return to the spirit of Saint Francis does not mean reverting to attitudes that characterized most of his contemporaries during the twelfth and thirteenth centuries. We cannot pretend ignorance of scientific procedures and self-righteously spurn technical possibilities. We cannot call technology a religious heresy and impose a superstitious dread of machines upon ourselves. That is not the point, since negativity toward something already negative is simply double discouragement—it is "nothing" compounded. The point of this discussion has been to find the secret of true riches. To do this, we must first perceive the actuality of evil behind its mask of promises. But, in the long run—in small things as in great—we must continue to embrace the positive.

Saint Francis loved physical poverty with all his heart, because it guarantees inner riches. It was his feeling that as he called less of this world his own, more of the world as a whole belonged to him. Lacking bodily raiment and shelter, he was clothed all the more intimately by cosmic weather; lacking food for his stomach, he was fed by the grace and beauty of the entire creation; lacking earthly power, he felt himself overflowing with currents of God's creativeness. Thus it was for Saint Francis. But the Lady Poverty he worshipped so gratefully and hopefully was not the same as our usual idea of poverty. She was simplicity of life and singleness of spirit—less *having* and more *being*. What afflicts us is the manifold craving to *have*—the seduction of our *being* due to our lust for *having*.

Until we have dug to the deepest cause of poverty, we cannot hope for its cure. That cause is identified in Christ's words: "To them that have shall be given, and from them that have not shall be taken, even what they have." To those that have what? "The kingdom of heaven is within," Christ said. "Seek first the kingdom of heaven, and all these things shall be added unto you." How shall we know the kingdom of heaven if not as the realm of intimate, eternal values? Where truth speaks and justice prevails, where spiritual beauty surrounds, and unselfish goodwill flows freely—there we must look for the kingdom that *should* come first, because it alone is self-sustaining and therefore capable also of sustaining humanity.

"To them that have shall be given" is the secret. Poverty swallows the "have-nots," and abundance awaits the "haves." To save humankind as a whole from technological impoverishment we must learn to convert have-nots into haves.

Picture two men walking along a road. Both are destitute, without job, home, money, or food. They have zero security and wealth. Yet one is a "have," the other a "have-not." The latter is gloomy, angry, and resentful. The other is glad for life, glad for sun and air, for kind thoughts that arise in his heart toward a bird singing. From inner fullness, despite his apparent nothing, he is ready to offer a friendly greeting, a listening ear, or a helping hand. We can easily imagine how, farther along, he will find friends, work, and cause to be thankful to life in ever new ways, whereas his companion on the road will probably continue to find life disappointing.

Like Saint Francis, we must remain open to the wellspring of gratitude for all the wonder and beauty of nature, for the good that is deepest in every human soul, for the joy in our ability to contemplate lovely thoughts and contribute acts of love. All these things are within the power of the poorest, who can show the way out of poverty. As thankfulness fills the heart, creative goodwill flows naturally, and favorable destiny comes to meet it.

If the reverent, thankful enjoyment of life is one's very ground of being and the secret of abundant destiny, then what is the scourge that renders this ground infertile? What hardens this earth and darkens the sun? What postpones the rain and makes its seeds lose incentive to grow? What scavenger eats the crops?

Such a scavenger is *despondency*, which is based on distrust of what lies beyond one's own control, Another is *disappointment*, which arises when personal wishes have not been fulfilled according to personal views of what is best. Yet another is blind *ambition*, which always places one's own good ahead of the concerns of others. These are all names for the enemy, and the family name is *egoism*.

The source of abundance is the God-filled universe itself, as long as it remains God-filled. The cause of impoverishment is alienation from that world of Being. We are alienated because each of us prefers to be the center of existence—a selfish god—and to make everything flow toward ourselves. If our sympathies were as universal as God's, there could be no harm, for our very being would support and enrich all of creation. But, initially, our sympathy is not universal. The more self-directed our consciousness becomes, the more self-seeking we become; the more self-seeking, the more limited; the more limited, the more impoverished. With great effort we try to possess all we can, no matter what the expense to others. Yet we begin to starve amid plenty. We are ignorant of, and thus unreceptive to, universal bounty. Our feeling of selfhood has not yet become a wellspring of creative love for all; until it becomes such a blessed fountain of being, it is drawn into the whirlpool of non-being.

Christ said, "Except a seed die, it shall not bring forth fruit." Modern human beings are slow to learn this secret of abundance. But to the extent that even one human being converts the craving of "All for me" into "I for all," the Earth will experience the end of one whirlpool and the beginning of one wellspring.

We are told that the craving of archetypal humankind at a certain stage of its formation in the "Garden of Eden" was to become as one of the gods. Eve and Adam were inspired by the serpent toward such self-aggrandizement through eating the fruit from the Tree of Knowledge. But their action was caused by the desire to *have*. They were not affirming the fruit of real existence but coveting it. They were pulling away from creative giving—which is the true secret of divine creativity—into selfish getting, which makes human beings in their immaturity the most rapacious of creatures. Adam was led to understand that until he and his companion could appreciate this difference, they and their successors would find themselves outside of abundance, cut off from real life, and walking the long road of poverty and pain.

At our present stage of development, whenever we gratefully manage to "see heaven in a grain of sand," we begin a change in direction that will gradually convert the impoverished Earth again into the abundant Garden. By seeing in this way, we begin to overcome egoism. Empty craving allows itself to be filled with the life that floods creative nature. Grateful love of all that wells up within overflows upon, enlivens, and enhances our surroundings. When with self-forgetfulness we turn our love toward the creation taking place around us, that same creative power arises within us as God's gift of "dominion." We shall ourselves become, out of our inexhaustible bounty, authentic givers to the whole universe.

The First Step toward Plenty

Thus far, we have looked in the most general way at life-orientations that enrich and ones that impoverish. Once we have discerned the difference, we can apply it to whatever confronts us, wherever we may be. Turning toward being and away from having does not require a different world; we can do it amid our present civilization. Particularly within the affluence of America, we can begin with gladness for all the gifts of convenience and comfort that come from technical achievements. The clarity and persistence of scientific effort warrants our warmest praise, The heroic will of business enterprise to overcome obstacles by applying scientific knowledge should stir our enthusiasm. In focusing on the positive— the first step toward plenty—we should continually remind ourselves of heroism of industrial pioneers, of their impressive characters and abilities. In trying to overcome scientific materialism, admiration for its real achievements is far less threatening than ignorance or indifference. Intimate knowledge of practical science allows us to appreciate with warm interest all that it has brought humankind through inner discipline as well as worldly goods. We do not need to fall under the spell of materialistic science, but we can approach it with a fully active spirit, which allows us genuine mastery over it.

To the extent that we can bring our *hearts* into science, it will be humanized. The danger of our time lies in the attitude that merely disavows existing conditions, wishing things were different. Such disgruntled passivity, based on illusions of high spirituality, is the materialism's closest ally. It is the final capitulation of human intelligence and purpose to what is inhuman.

The transformation of industrial society is a task for adults who have decided to be as good to nature as nature has been to them, to bless nature through moral achievements and enactment as much as nature has blessed them with its bounty. We must all root ourselves better in the soil where we stand. As far as economic theory and attitudes go, the roots of our thinking and feeling must press beyond the hardpan of selfishness—the profit motive. We must recognize that whenever we work (with or without machines) primarily for what we ourselves get out of the work, we contribute to impoverishment in general.

Each small whirlpool of greed, added to all the others, helps to make society into a great whirlpool of scarcity, drawing the world's abundance so that, eventually, it will benefit none. Individual enterprise, freedom, and responsibility are the creative side of the human I. These qualities should be strengthened and increased. Providing *first for oneself*, on the other hand, is consumptive and impoverishing. Adam Smith's laws will not prevent poverty and strife in the wake of the egos thus motivated.

To build a better society for the future—based on more grateful, reverent, and generous attitudes—is the task awaiting our children now in school. In my book *Education in Search of the Spirit*,[10] I have suggested that, by approaching knowledge in a new way, we can begin to help children find a loving attitude toward life. Ultimately, it is love that makes the difference between those that have and those that have not.

---

10. See footnote, p.12.

10.

THE SECRET OF PEACE

*Peace is not absence of war; it is a virtue born
out of the strength of the heart.* —Spinoza

MANY IDEALISTIC YOUNG Americans are profoundly dis-
turbed about their country's involvement in war after war.
They do not see how one can love a homeland that seems unwilling to take an absolute stand against war. At one time perhaps war served a noble purpose, but in our time it is no
longer valid.

Many idealists, both old and young, are so ardently in favor
of a permanent peace, and so incensed against those who permit the continuation of war, that they often fail to perceive
something about themselves that is also true. They may fail to
observe the extent of their own belligerence, which is the cause
of war. Convinced that war can never establish peace—any
more than Satan will cast out Satan—such people remain unaware that militant pacifism is unlikely to achieve peace.

In trying to think through the fallacy of militant pacifism
without promoting the cause of war, my thoughts have con-
densed into a surprising axiom: War is a function of those
who think in twos; peace is made by those who think in
threes. This expresses much that goes to the heart of the question of peace today.

As a person thinks in the heart, so that person will be. And as a person thinks, so that person's world eventually becomes—one's personal life, social institutions, and the whole environment. One who has the mental habit of thinking in dualities can expect life's experience to arrange themselves in opposing camps. Such a person should not be surprised, when looking around, to see strife and conflict. Inevitably, one is drawn into conflict by holding onto the dualistic concepts of good and bad; not only are the facts and forces of one's environment at war with one another, but such a person will also be engaged as a part of these wars. The dualistic individual will see one side of any given battle as good, the other as bad and will feel compelled to fight for the good against the bad.

Most of us tend to view the world, to some degree, in such dualities. We have been educated to do so, and we will no doubt continue in this way until we comprehend the warlike implications of dualism and the usual thinking underlying it. Real peace will become possible when psychologists, ministers, doctors, and teachers recognize the necessity of going beyond customary knowledge.

Modern education is based on the intellect. It rewards the mentally precocious. It's goal is to strengthen the power of critical judgment in students and to habituate them to the analytical procedures of natural science. Even the semi-educated become intellectuals. Thus, education prepares us for war: war among nations, classes, sects, and races. We are prepared for war in marriage, between the generations, and between humankind and nature.

This must have been part of what Rudolf Steiner meant in 1919 when he made a prediction. During the exhaustion following World War One, when all of humanity was looking forward to a lasting peace, Steiner said, "The schools only have to continue teaching as they do now, and in thirty years the world will again be in flames." This became evident in 1939.

It is characteristic of the intellectual mind that its inquiry proceeds by isolating facts—discriminating among possibilities, distinguishing this from that, and then subdividing it. The leaf is separated from the stalk for study, then the chlorophyll is separated from the leaf and the chloroplast from the chlorophyll. Scientific investigation, which is simply a systematic application of intellect, proceeds by "digging" into things. Its driving wedge makes the first split, and this split is followed by others. This process has lead to the refining of oil, the splitting of the atom, and the confounding of human society. Analysis even sets one against oneself.

If intellectual science did *not* split phenomena, it would be stopped in its tracks. It would be rendered helpless. It could do nothing and make no contribution—only stare dumbly at the world. Science can proceed only by making further distinctions—that is, by more splitting. When analysis is suspended, scientific interest dies along with its power to inform; as F. Georg Juenger says in his *Failure of Technology*, "The intellect is incapable of comprehending an indivisible whole."[1]

Yet an alternate possibility exists that is occasionally used: through deeper attentiveness, scientists *can*, without digging and splitting, allow the phenomenon in its original unity to awaken a deeper realization in the soul. The soul then experiences another mode of knowing. We may call this other mode *intuition*, the comprehension of a being in its integrity and living presence. Intuition experiences the phenomenon precisely in its indivisible oneness.

---

1. F. Georg Juenger, *The Failure of Technology*, op. cit.

One, Two, and Three

What can numbers, as symbols, tell us about intellect and intuition? They can help us understand how we came to develop science as it is today, and how we may progress beyond its fatal end-result—war.

Modern science is the result of a very long historical development. If we feel the reality behind the language of religious myth, we may recognize that the quest for knowledge began in Paradise, or the Garden of Eden. When Adam ate prematurely of the Tree of Knowledge, he awakened to the manifest material world but, as a result, began to fall asleep spiritually. He began to acquire intellect and to lose intuition. The gradual triumph of intellectuality that began with Adam is modern science.

The Paradise condition may be symbolized by *One*; the Fall from Paradise by *Two*. Intellect was born under the sign of Two. Because of the egoism of reaching prematurely for "knowledge," humanity came into conflict with the heavenly source, was ejected, and entered the experience of Two. Driven from the home enjoyed in the intuitive unity of spiritual consciousness, human beings found themselves confronting the Earth and its creatures with a different, "fallen" consciousness. Thereafter, they had to till and master the Earth as strangers to it, in pain and by the sweat of their brows. Because our whole experience was split asunder, we have from that time on come to view all circumstances of earthly existence as good or evil.

Tradition tells us that in Paradise human beings understood the language of bird and beast. They were nourished gratuitously. They lived in joy and at one with their surroundings. The human soul lived in all, and all lived in it; the divine creative principle was experienced as All in all. This All is expressed in the number One. Humanity had been at home in the eternal, but could no longer live there and descended into time. Human beings could look to the past and future and be torn between the two. They could look upon Earth and up to heaven, and feel torn between the two. Man and wife confronted each other as strangers. Humanity was closed off from the Nature of nature, regarding every being from the outsider's standpoint; every will would now contest every other will. All this is implied in the number Two.

Whereas tradition tells us that humanity once dwelled in the Paradise of One and was expelled to wander, worry, and work in the torment of Two, another tradition predicts how humanity will end if it fails to master this dualism, which sets each human I-being against the world. This other tradition predicts that those who do not sufficiently muster the desire to go beyond the Two will have to experience dualism in its ultimate form—the holocaust that Hobbes called the "war of all against all."

In the fullness of time, Providence has opened the way out of Two, but as individuals we must recognize and choose to go this new way. The path of human development should not, however, lead us back from Two to One but forward to Three, which is the *new* One. Three might represent peace after war, or conflict transformed into the creative—in other words, the road to Paradise Regained.

As modern people we are currently immersed in materialism, and the organ for material cognition is the intellect, which separates everything. We must use this intellect, of course, yet we must also master and transcend it. If we are to move toward the future under the sign of Three, we must accept the usefulness of the intellectual distinctions and see them as both arising *from* and capable of returning *into* unities. Such unity can be known only through intuition.

We should not attempt, in our quest for peace, to unify, to reject modern intelligence and revert to primordial consciousness; we should instead strengthen intuition until, in a modern way, it can hold its own in relation to our intellect. Complete cognition requires us to maintain a balance between these two faculties. When they supplement each other, we can fully experience reality, knowing both the inner and the outer natures of things—creative being and created fact. By comprehending the unity in multiplicity we can give our attention equally to either.

The Heart As Center

In his *Tractatus Politicus*, Spinoza says, "Peace is not the absence of war; it is a virtue born out of the strength of the heart." This sounds promising, but what does it really mean? Not much light is shed on this through the sentimental feeling that heart-things are "good" things, and peace is a "good" thing, therefore peace must be of the heart. To know how the heart serves peace, we must be aware of the heart's role in the human being.

The heart is placed centrally in the human body—approximately in the center between top and bottom, left and right, front and back. This does not seem accidental, since the heart functions as a mediator. As the central organ of the ever-moving blood system, the heart actively mediates between the activities in the head and in the abdomen—between the impalpable world of sensation and cerebration above and the substantial world of digestion, assimilation and propagation below.

Since the head is the rounded observatory that humankind thrusts up toward the heavens, and the feet are the platform turned toward the Earth, we may view the human being as living between Heaven and Earth, and the flow of heart's blood as uniting the experience of these two worlds. The blood moves between thought and action. At the synapses of the nerves, blood approaches matters of consciousness; through the *villi* of the small intestine it receives the nourishment for bodily growth. Within the *alveoli* of the lungs, the blood replaces death with life. In the liver cells it assists in discriminating what will be built up from what will be destroyed. The blood maintains the balance between conditions of hot and cold, acidic and alkaline, instability and stability. If we allow ourselves poetic truth, we would probably not be far from doctor's truth by saying that the blood mediates constantly, rhythmically, and creatively between sympathy and antipathy, awake and asleep, life and death, Heaven and Earth.

The heart, as the focus and master of the flowing blood, is between opposite extremes of all kinds. The coursing of the blood and the opening and closing of the blood vessels—mostly those of the heart—can be viewed as creative interactions that allow opposite realities to alternately dominate in the right rhythm. Through this yea-saying and nay-saying, opposing substances, forces, and tendencies successively contribute to the good of the whole without becoming too recessive or dominant. The health of the whole being increases as a third reality through the alternating acceptance and rejection of the heart's blood, just as the human body moves forward along a straight course that is neither that of the left leg nor that of the right one, but that of both of them working in rhythmical sequence, each making its limited progress and giving way to the other.

Whether or not in the opinion of modern medical knowledge we have stretched certain points in imagining the role of the blood and heart in human beings, we can very well use our blood system to symbolize how the Three properly overcomes the Two. We can visualize what Spinoza meant by the virtue of peace being born of a heart strong enough to do its work. Those of us who would make peace are between opposing extremes of many kinds, and we must know—not just instinctively but consciously—how to avoid the confrontation and combat that exists between them. We must introduce a third element by artfully validating opposing aspects while reconciling those opposites.

The Sign of Three

More than peace is indicated by the sign of Three. Every virtue, every good, stands under the same sign. When the truth of this is seen, the possibility and insurance of peace exist. When, however, good is the preferred half of a duality, war will be certain in the long run.

As dualists, for example, we see a particular good opposed to a particular evil; we believe, in general, that good is opposed to evil. We imagine that courage stands against cowardice, love against hate, truth against falsehood, and so on. But when we see life in terms of Three, we regard matters differently. We then never place good in an extreme position—as equal and opposite to any particular evil—but raise it above the two evils below, which are always polarized. We comprehend that the true good results precisely from the *constructive working* together of these two opposing "evils." The art of life is to achieve the good by walking the middle way and not allowing oneself to be drawn out of balance.

Left and right, height and depth, become evils only when we allow them to distort us from our centrality. So long as we hold the position of mastery, we can regard opposing powers as potentialities for good. By drawing them into our service instead of allowing ourselves to be drawn into theirs, we actualize the good. We become grateful rather than inimical toward what helps our progress toward goodness and truth.

Young men and women are becoming more and more polarized and radicalized today on social questions. They imagine, first, that there are only two real positions to take in any dispute; second, that only one of these is right; and third, that the most abhorrent position is the intermediate one, since this constitutes the "no-man's" land of doubt and indecision. Intellectuals think that to give continuing credence to both sides of a question is to hang helplessly between them. Validating both sides requires courage in the face of the unknown, as well as the will to create something out of nothing, and neither of these strengths is characteristic of the intellectual. As intellectuals, we tend to feel our selfhood only within opposition; by locking ourselves into the stance of a fixed opinion, by giving over our living judgment to the authority of an abstract principle, we gain a false sense of self-existence.

To see potential for good on both sides of every question without identifying with either requires what Paul Tillich called "the courage to be"; we are stimulated in the depths of our being, and our emptiness is filled, through the creative interweaving of opposites. The failure to take such a step is true indecision.

There is a real difference between progressively and regressively overcoming dualities, or the warfare of opposites. Black, or the principle of darkness, for example, is at the opposite pole from white, the principle of light. Is the median position grey? It need not be. It could be a color, according to Goethe. The whole world of glowing color is born out of the interplay of light and darkness. Grey does not really mediate between light and darkness but cancels both and replaces them with something less vivid than either. Color, on the other hand, is a new and more vivid creation. As Goethe said, it arises from the interaction of light with darkness when both work in their full vitality.

Male is opposed to female, and vice versa. "Compromise" would neuter both aspects and produce nothing. Marriage, however, brings forth a child born of love. Father and mother call into existence the child who will go beyond them.

The secret of Three is that it converts destructive antagonism into constructive cooperation. Only free human beings consciously wield this secret. In this way they produce the genuinely new, and they can do so because they begin with nothing already in existence. In every dichotomy one dynamic exists, and its opposite also exists. One who yields to either is borne up and carried on its particular current. We engage ourselves properly and achieve virtue by mingling both dynamics according to freely imagining the creation of what does not yet exist.

Every virtue arises from the principle of Three. As mentioned, it is false to imagine that courage is merely the opposite of fear, love the opposite of hate, and truth the opposite of lies. Experience shows us that we do not become courageous simply by abandoning fear; without fear we become foolhardy. Eliminating antipathy does not necessarily produce love; without antipathy, which is necessary for every objective evaluation, we become fatuous in our sympathies.

Scrupulous adherence to observed facts is not truth. Truth expresses reality when two cognitive principles are employed: *observation*, which perceives, and *intuition*, which conceives. *Percept* and *concept* are not given together, nor do they flow together automatically on their own. They must be brought together through the human will. Truth requires fidelity to observed facts; it also requires the creative effort of interpretation. Truth is found when outer evidence confirms the inner, and when inner testimony illumines the outer. Truth requires both the outer and the inner component.

In the matter of courage, self-assertion, based on our confidence in what we intend, and self-negation based on our anxiety about what the world portends, are brought into living balance by courage. Courage does not cancel fear but uses it.

And one cannot love, so long as one is irresistibly drawn by sympathy for another being. Although such attractions are often considered to be love and become the basis for marriage, they are really compulsions, and the resulting marriages eventually suffer the opposite compulsion. Instinct naturally tries to correct for imbalance, and therefore compulsory desire will lead to habitual, cold antagonism. This sequence is what psychologists have in mind when they speak of love as ambivalent. True love, however, is unequivocal. It exists wherever free souls are able to balance sympathy and antipathy. To young people who are trying to distinguish between true and false love one would like to advise that the heart's real heart opens only when the urge toward self-abandonment is countered by equally strong self-recollection and self-recovery. This truth comes to anyone who sufficiently develops the strength of single-minded idealism to withstand the manifold aspects of desire.

Spiritual versus Material

Let us consider how a triadic conception would deal with certain other dualities. One is spiritual versus material; another is selfishness versus unselfishness, or egoism versus altruism.

When religious thought places spirituality in opposition to material existence, people become unwilling to make the cause of the spirit their own. They fail to do their best to become spiritual because they cannot love a state of being that negates their whole existence on Earth. Certainly such people do not love materialism, since it weighs them down and robs life of dignity and beauty. Just as deeply, however, they distrust a pietistic spirituality, for it tends to undermine the value of material existence. People feel that coping with immersion in material existence is the essence of the human drama. Christ said, "Be *in* the world, though not of the world"; but if the goodness of spirit consists of making war against matter and viewing it as bad, then that "goodness" should try to weaken earth-life, empty it, and shorten it by every means possible. One should not be in the world at all. What good can it serve to linger in a bad camp?

Christ's word, however, indicates that the meaning of life, or the virtue of it, requires us as spiritual beings to enter sympathetically into the world of matter, to understand it, give it love and—taking it by the hand—lift it out of its enchantment. Thus did Christ himself set the example, and in this his teaching differs from much of traditional Eastern thought.

When spirit is set against matter in the form of good against evil and truth against illusion, modern Western people cannot accept the spiritual path. Our proper instinct tells us that worldly experience is more an opportunity than an illusion. Westerners long for spirit, certainly, but will not give themselves wholeheartedly to any spiritual advice or system that considers it necessary to oppose material reality. There is the sense that one must simply manage as well as possible between a distaste for materialism and a distrust of spirituality. How different it would be if those who represent a true, modern spiritual life could simply agree that world-estranged spirituality is just as bad as spirit-estranged materialism. They would then respond to a way of development that seeks neither the world-alienating spirit nor the spirit-alienating world, but instead endeavors to interpenetrate these two principles, since each has something essential to contribute to the other.

As we have said, it is a sound instinct that tells both Easterners and Westerners today that human nature properly indentifies itself always with the evolving middle term that lies between but above opposites.

Egoism and Altruism

The conflict between egoism and altruism is fundamental to each of us and is often discussed within political, economic, and religious contexts. Generally, we view altruism as good and egoism as bad. Equally often, few of us attempt to make this good our own—that is, to become completely "unselfish." Privately, we feel somehow justified in pursuing our own interest, though our dualistic moral views look on with a frown.

Outwardly, we are similarly unregenerate. Within the context of social theory, for example, although many maintain that free enterprise in economics and nationalism in politics are egoistic and hence undesirable, and although a socialist economy and a world government are frequently proposed as being altruistic and desirable, a profound instinct still prevents a majority in the West from trying to be "good" in such respects. We remain unconvincing.

We admit that, for human society and the planet whose bounty we enjoy, there is something very unwholesome about the way enterprisers tend to become exploiters. This is also true of the way nationalism leads to bloodshed. Yet we are simply not persuaded that to love one's homeland is reprehensible or should be wiped out by the ideal of internationalism. In the matter of socialism, too, we are skeptical about any economy's chances of prospering when the so-called altruistic political apparatus takes over what it does not understand.

The solution of the riddle of warring dualities is always the same. The Greeks and the Buddhists found it in their "middle way" and their "nothing in excess." The English have practiced it in their national habit of "muddling through". Thus, my purpose in proposing the advance from the sign of Two to the sign of Three has not been to claim a "new discovery."

In terms of human development, egoism is bad, but so is altruism when it goes too far. Placing too much emphasis on either the self or the world has bad consequences for both. If we habitually place ourselves first, we are experienced by others as overbearing and obnoxious. Despite our own illusion of size and worth, we actually begin to shrink. The resulting emptiness becomes boring even to ourselves.

On the other hand, when forgetting the self is carried to an extreme, one is swept away by the world. By committing ourselves too hastily, we cannot carry through. Indecision, error, and illness follow over-extension. We prove to the world our own lack of what we should offer—a resourceful, vital, intact I-being.

As small individual selves, we cannot respond to all of the vast world in which we exist nor assume more than our healthy share of responsibility. We must limit our sense of obligation and even our awareness. Whereas it is virtuous and beautiful to give our lives to the support of universal ideals, such an offering requires an intact, intelligent life to give—otherwise, our gift lacks the necessary value. One's own development must be considered, because personal strength is needed to properly re-alize universal ideals.

The healthy individual advances to meet and embrace the world, which will call out what is deepest in the self; yet one does not hesitate at times to place the self first, if such self-enhance-ment will make it stronger and wiser for service to the world.

War and Peace, Life and Death

Let us now apply the sign of Three to the issue of war and peace. Peace, said Spinoza, is not the absence of war. It is also not the opposite of war. By simply opposing war *in principle*, we cannot imagine that we are peace-makers. Perhaps we are really war-makers, since we merely create a new duality and stand on one side or the other. We make war against war and call it a peace effort. Real peace, however, arises only when the two principles at odds are constructively reconciled—both ac-knowledged and used, neither of them dominant or sup-pressed. The principles themselves may oppose each other, but peace does not really oppose either of them. It looks beyond their opposition and draws them both into service.

Some young idealists may have followed this line of reasoning sympathetically up to this point, yet balk when their ideal of peace is allocated to the number two, the war-making, position. They might wonder how it can possibly be considered that an all-out campaign for the immediate cessation of war is a dubious endeavor.

The vehement certainty of some who think they are striving for peace is based on an over-simplification. They believe that war means killing people, and that peace means saving people's lives. Life, they feel, is an indispensable good; death, an irreme-diable evil. The perspective that "life is good and death is bad" is another example of how dualism is at odds with reality. Those of great wisdom throughout history have recognized that life, when it does not sacrifice itself, is not real life: "For whoever saves one's own life shall lose it." And the death of a brave, loyal, honest person is by no means obliteration or defeat. "Spirit dies to become human," Novalis said; and "the human dies to become spirit." Or as the enigmatic and profound Heraclitus said, two thousand years earlier: "Mortals are immortals, and immortals are mortals, each living the death and dying the life of the other."

Death is not the "final obscenity," as we sometimes hear these days. There are certainly many cases—including death in battle—when death becomes a human being's highest achievement and the cornerstone of a blessed new beginning. If one insists upon understanding life materialistically, however, one will misunderstand every aspect of it, and above all the riddle of life and death.

To say that peace as mere absence of war should *not* be an ideal, is to say, in terms of our discussion, that such a peace can be just as destructive as war; both are one-sided. Yet both serve good when they are woven together properly by a still higher principle—the *higher* principle that Spinoza called "true peace."

Whether from the viewpoint of culture, nation, or individual, peace as mere absence of war can come to mean passive self-indulgence, fear, and forgetfulness of the highest goals. Despite its obvious benefits, mere peace may mean the absence of any shock adequate to dislodge selfish habits, unsound thinking, comfort, security, pleasure, and life itself. Mere peace can permit great aberrations in personal and social conduct to go unchecked, because no tool that merely protects one's own life is strong and sharp enough to prune them. Through this kind of peace people can lose their souls.

War, on the other hand—despite the grief and devastation it wreaks upon individuals and nations, and despite the brutality and hate it unleashes in many human souls—has for other souls been an opportunity to clarify issues, discover their deepest hidden strengths, and summon absolute courage in order to open the way to entirely new and better beginnings. In spite of its horrors, there has been something in war that leavens even as it purges and disciplines. Many nations have been powerfully renewed through the sacrifice its loyal citizens have made in battle.[2]

In speaking this way of war, I am not referring to the violent assault of a calculating despot. Sheer aggression, regardless of the cause, brings the heavy fate of counter-aggression upon the perpetrators. In the whole history of war the majority of those who have done the fighting and dying have done so for honor, duty, and love of their homeland, in the spirit of loyalty to comrades and respect for authority. To the extent that these motives do in fact predominate over brutal instincts in those who are called to war, the latter achieve something of greatest value for themselves and for their country. When we look at war in this light, both sides appear honorable, both feel justified, and both achieve a certain moral advancement that counters much that has not been honorable. To imagine, much less judge, the infinitely complex web of moral value and accountability in any particular war—woven of the dark and bright threads of many levels—probably exceeds human

---

2. Admiral Richard E. Byrd, also made this point: "But the peace I describe is not passive. It must be won. Real peace comes from struggle that involves such things as effort, discipline, enthusiasm. This is also the way to strength. An inactive peace may lead to sensuality and flabbiness, which are discordant. It is often necessary to fight to lessen discord. This is the paradox," *Alone*, G. P. Putnam's Sons, New York, 1938, p. 162.

ability. We need not pass judgment on the whole significance of war but we may affirm a single positive aspect of it. This aspect is generally not considered by those whose otherwise laudable pacifism is too simply conceived.

An analogy may be useful here. We fear sickness and usually try to avoid it. Yet it often serves a purpose, which may be detected by an impartial observer. When we fail to solve a life-problem through conscious effort, it takes hold of us below consciousness. We become engaged instinctively and organically. Inadequate thoughts, unsound feelings, an immorality may be corrected by direct attention, but if they are not, it seems that the organism itself will be put to the test. The consequences of error are then fought at the bodily level through fever and pain, but essentially with positive gains.

Through fever and pain we purge maladies that would otherwise foreclose all further development. We are thus forced to summon what is deepest in us, to throw off what had begun to burden and darken the spirit. It is well known to doctors, for example, that the high fevers accompanying infectious diseases can be an antidote to degenerative tendencies in the organism. We can observe how the incidence of degenerative illnesses, such as cancer, arteriosclerosis, arthritis, and mental disease, have gotten out of control at the very time when, through vaccines and antibiotics, we have succeeded in suppressing many kinds of infection. A sentimental observer might think that the goal of medicine should be to prevent all sickness as soon as possible, but it would be disastrous if this means of fighting for our lives were removed before moral and psychological errors have also been eliminated.

Sound medicine tries to avoid or moderate illness, just as diplomats try to avoid war or mitigate its horrors. Although such strenuous efforts are necessary, so long as there is hope for humankind there will be no absolute prevention of sickness or war until evil and error are overcome.

Unequivocal praise of peace and absolute condemnation of war bring to mind an older tradition that viewed the sacrifice of life through war as the last hope of preventing something worse than war. This could be called *moral materialism.* According to this ancient belief, if it were not for the hardship, suffering, and death caused by wars, accidents, and natural catastrophes, a materialistically inclined society would soon become thoroughly degenerate. As the human spirit begins to be touched with higher realities, and the human will suffers a paralyzing lack of enthusiasm and conviction, a demonic lust and cruelty, depravity and malice, begin to prevail.

It is remarkable that, in our age of widespread materialism, millions of human beings nevertheless retain real warmth and friendliness and a wholesome desire for what is noble and good, as well as some reverence for a higher order of reality. Do we perhaps owe much of this grace to the blood sacrifice of those on both sides of the battle front who, in the past, perished innocently in war?

If, without scorning or twisting the meaning of this ancient idea, we consider that there is truth in it, we may believe that although war has in some respects always been monstrous and dreadful (and even more so today), peace as mere suppression of war could conceivably wreak still deeper havoc. When the icy shroud of materialism burdens existence, the fire of war breaks forth as a kind of spiritual necessity to melt that ice.

The Moral Equivalent of War

What higher principle can we imagine that works creatively to weave together what is potentially good in peace as the treasure of a noble life, and in war as the treasure of a noble death? This question brings us to a formula that may indicate the whole meaning of life. The life worth living broadens *self-* interest every moment to embrace what it loves more than it- self. It subdues attachment to its own life in order to know and support what will prosper the life of others. By sacrificing personal bias, it comes closer to a beauty, goodness, and truth that is objective and universal. In such transcendence of self, life is actually fulfilled.

We may say, therefore, that our personal abilities and achievements are the treasure of our life, that the universal spir- it that animates us is the treasure of our death. In this sense, death fructifies life. "Those who do not die before dying, when they die putrefy," said the mystic. If people fight the battle of ordinary life within themselves in such a way that they risk and lose their lives daily for ideals, then they no longer need phys- ical war. By accepting the lifelong danger, adventure, and mor- tal challenge of this battle within themselves, human beings will win the creative death-in-life and life-in-death that exist high above any "peaceful life" based on mere fear of death.

As we enter the twenty-first century, we must ask ourselves why those who are rational, orderly, scientific, and communi- cative as never before in history, were hurled twice within the span of a few years into world wars of unprecedented violence and overwhelming destructiveness. Why should such vicious fires continue to spring up and burn tenaciously, one after an- other, constantly threatening to break into total conflagration? Is something fundamental trying to express itself? Is there an unknown impulse arising from the depths of human souls—an irresistible force that is being blocked by an immovable wall? Could this as yet unrecognized impulse be the will to make sci- ence, art, religion, and all forms of human relationships finally responsible to the true human spirit? Are the obstacles to this impulse an immense inertia and a great fear—the blockage of old ways of thinking that go back for many hundreds, perhaps thousands, of years?

We could have been spared the revolutions of the youth, the breakdown of law and morality, the destruction of nature, and the threat of more terrible holocausts, if we had identified and welcomed the changes necessary for humankind to retain its humanity and fulfill its task on Earth. But our science, religion, education, and many of our social structures have remained stuck in ways that became obsolete long ago, thus two things had to happen: Our situation had to worsen until even the most blind could begin to see the problem; and there had to be a powerful shake-up. Are we at last shaken down to fundamentals? We can hope so but hardly expect it. We avoid further warfare only if we get serious enough to overcome the fear, greed, self-indulgence, and conceit that persistently blind us to the necessity for a revolution in our whole way of understanding.

War is a radical principle, whereas peace is conservative, but whenever peace serves only to preserve the old, humanity has turned to war—at least partly out of longing for needed change. War loses this elemental, undeniable appeal when peace also becomes *creative*—that is, when humanity achieves a peace based on the inner principle of "Die and become!"

The realization that war and ordinary peace are opposites because of their one-sidedness—each partially good and partially bad—is to become aware of the necessity for a third principle that can draw a positive contribution from each side. This third principle allows *Life* with a capital *L* and *Peace* with a capital *P*. This *Life* advances by curbing ordinary life; and this *Peace* prospers by sacrificing ordinary peace. It brings us to what William James saw as the only peaceful adventure that could satisfy an otherwise recurring appetite for war. His "moral equivalent of war" is a life of peace, whose every moment involves spiritual activity, self-knowledge, and self-conquest. In the life of mortal challenge that is true peace, the creative spirit in humanity works for the upward transformation of the whole Earth, upon which it is graced to live.

11.

LEADERSHIP IN EDUCATION

THE WORLDWIDE, faculty-run school movement with which I have long been connected, has come to view the concept of "leadership" with a caution bordering on rejection. In a recent internationally distributed guide to the philosophy and methodology of this school fellowship, one section attempts to explain "How a school functions without a director." It opens with a simple question: "It is often said that a school is as good as its head teacher; so, what if there isn't one?"[1]

This question is intended to challenge the usual assumption that leadership is necessary to the health of every educational institution—in the person of a head teacher, principal, or director. The argument against this supposition by the guidebook includes a chart of the complex interactions of teacher and parent committees. It is presumed that they can handle any problems that can arise in a harmonious, efficient school. They are composed of committed individuals of good will

---

1. *Waldorf Educaton Exhibition Catalog*, Freunde der Erziehungskunst Rudolf Steiners, Stuttgart, 1994, pp. 70–71.

who work as equals and avoid being subordinate to any superior authority.

The brief passage referred to ends with a statement of conviction, expressed in a way that presumes to speak for all schools of this orientation:

> Responsibility and freedom are two interconnected qualities that permeate and determine how a Waldorf school works: through the principles of autonomy and consensus, rather than through autocracy and hierarchy.

In the matter of leadership, what is it that distinguishes an idealistic school from, say, a symphony orchestra, opera, or choir—or a sound business or political organization? All these enterprises feel the necessity for and welcome strong leadership. Experience tells them that leaders fill an essential role.

A musical conductor may have less opportunity to enjoy playing the particular instruments in the orchestra than do the musicians being directed. This is also true for a choral director. Why don't mature orchestras, operas, and choirs manage their affairs, then, solely on the basis of group consensus and individual autonomy? Why do the very best musicians and actors gravitate precisely toward the strongest conductors and directors, gladly placing themselves under such leadership? Political organizations, businesses, and religious congregations generally hope for strong leadership, from whom they willingly accept corrective discipline as well as creative encouragement.

Does such desire for and submission to leadership express weakness? Does it set up hierarchy and autocracy? We need to clarify the meaning of such words as *leadership, hierarchy*, and *authority*. We need to understand the relationship between the genuine, firm, and respected authority of true leaders and the autonomy and creative freedom that result for those who willingly listen and obey.

Authority

Is the leader who exercises decisive authority an autocrat? No doubt, *some* who are chosen as leaders tend to make the most of such authority by becoming autocratic—that is, demanding and dictatorial. Where is the difference between a desirable, wholesome, and rewarding leadership, and the kind that is counterproductive because it betrays its intended role?

Leadership implies an authority that supervises and helps guide a community of individuals. Yet the genuine leader of such a community is not necessarily the most skilled regarding all the specific functions and problems that face that group. Is there such a thing as a special ability to facilitate harmonious, creative collaboration? How is this function to be conceived?

In any field, the matter of spirit—its presence or absence—is fundamental to the question of leadership. The ability to heed and serve the living spirit of any endeavor calls for a rare combination of supple flexibility and steadfast integrity. Sometimes leaders are characterized as too flexible and fluid or, on the other hand, too rocklike and adamant. Yet both qualities are needed in higher degrees than usual. It is the mark of true leadership that it can justify and embrace apparently irreconcilable viewpoints and behaviors, just as great composers give play to strong contrasts in their music and then, through their talent for counterpoint, resolve them in the service of harmony.

Saint John recounts the most perfect example of the relationship between high power and lowly service. Surrounded by His disciples, Christ Jesus removed His outer garments and, girt only with a towel, knelt before those whom He has led. As He washed the feet of each, wiping them dry with a towel, they were nonplused and asked, "Why are you doing this? You are our Master and Lord!" Jesus replied, "You call me Master and Lord; and you say well, for so I am. If I, your Lord and Master, have washed your feet, you should also wash one another's feet. For I have given you an example, that you should do as I have done to you" (John 13:3–17).

Jesus said, in other words: It is true that I am hierarchically above you, but I am commissioning you yourselves now to go forth in turn. You will in a sense be hierarchically above those whom you will be allowed to lead. And when that time comes, do not fail to remember my example. It is offered you as the archetype and essence of all leadership. If I have knelt before you to wash your feet—including the one who will betray me—remember that, when you are raised up as leaders, you too must never regard yourselves as superior, but must kneel naked as I have done, in humblest service to your followers. As I have laid aside my clothes, so must you lay aside your security, habit, convenience, and pride—if, as you serve, you would do the will of the spirit world above you.

The path to excellence in leadership is through service. *Serving* is the creative goal of all who love. What makes both teachers and leaders effective is the ability to awaken the virtues that await in those whom they are privileged to serve. And those being taught and led—who do not consider themselves weak or blind followers—are presented an opportunity to develop their own independent courage and creative initiative. The interest, compassion, and service that emanates from true teachers and leaders are the spiritual goods they transmit to those who follow them. The strengths present in those who are able to offer loving guidance will always arouse the same qualities in those who choose to be taught and led.

Emerson states:

> The world has been instructed by its kings, who have magnetized the eyes of nations. It has been taught by this colossal symbol the reverence due from man to man. The *joyful loyalty* with which men everywhere suffered the king, the noble, or the great proprietor to walk among them by a law of his own [representing] the law in his person, was the hieroglyphic by which they obscurely signified their consciousness of their own right and comeliness: the right of every man. (Emphasis added) [2]

This quotation should indeed be taken to imply that, whereas kings may once have had a role to play, it served only to awaken the realization that *every* human being deserves the highest respect. We the people have come into our own and, therefore, the time for kings is past. On the other hand, Emerson could also be understood as saying that the day for real kings, or leaders, will never pass, because those who freely follow will always be awakened and strengthened by their leader's "hieroglyphic" example. The whole function of leaders, now as always, is *to elevate* rather than subordinate those they serve—from whom and for whom they have accepted their high responsibility.

Hierarchy

Examples of genuine hierarchy show that such ordering and ranking are found everywhere. It is an inevitable feature of life itself. Indeed, *hierarchy* is simply another term for the essence

---

2. Emerson, "Self-Reliance."

of all evolution. Hierarchical development simply implies the advance from lower to higher stages. This advance is the very goal and glory of life itself. Think of the presence and bearing of mountains. Every high mountain stands on a dark, submerged base that alone makes possible its ascent to the summit encircled by air and light. This same analogy applies also to the hierarchical rise of a mighty tree. In both cases the humble, deep descent into Earth's darkness of the mountain's base and the tree's roots makes possible the rise of a crown in the opposite direction, toward the heavens.

So it is with us human beings. Because our feet are planted so definitely on the lowly earth, our heads are able to rise most nobly toward the stars above. Intellectually speaking, our heads seem to represent highest consciousness, and to this end the brain up in the head is our body's most refined and useful member. Yet, the ascendancy of the physical brain, with its clear consciousness, indeed presupposes that our human feet are more decisively placed down below on the earth than is true of even the highest members of the animal kingdom.

The concept of hierarchy, in whatever sense, should not be understood one-sidedly. Here, as elsewhere, we see that first appearances can lead to serious misunderstanding. What we find, in one sense, to be *physically* highest—the nerve centers in the head—are found to be the lowest in their ability to support truly high spiritual consciousness. And what we rank physically lowest—the organs of metabolism, procreation, and movement—are *potentially* the highest. Thus, the human consciousness served by the brain and sensory nerves—where they are the bodily instruments of brightness, as it were—seems to have the capacity to know most truly. But the content of head consciousness is only the result of sensations drawn from the purely physical world, or the abstract, intellectual concepts that attempt to organize and interpret sensory experience. The imponderable spirit living creatively and formatively in all things is not found by either the brain or the physical senses. It allows us to approached only through a higher consciousness, which ordinarily lies sleeping below in the heart and lungs, housed in the chest. Physically, these organs are as far below the skull-housed brain and physical senses as they are above the abdominal organs, legs, and feet. When a more spiritual consciousness awakens, it moves toward cognitive use of these intermediate organs, because, being central, they have the ability to reconcile what is above with what is below. They open to both higher and deeper truths than are conveyed by the physical senses and brain alone. Consciousness at this level awakens to the actual immediacy of spiritual life, penetrating beyond the closed mystery of material facts, physically perceived and conceived. Here it awaits still more profound intuition of the depths.

When the transforming power of human consciousness descends even farther, to spiritual organs in the region physically lowest of all, it actually rises to become aware of its reality in a cosmic sense, altogether beyond the physical. It comes to know itself as something that did not begin with physical conception and will not end with physical death. From this region of the lowest, most dynamic centers of life in the human organism, a wholly intuitive, altogether transcendent experience of spiritual realities is released.

Thus, *hierarchy* reverses itself, while remaining hierarchical. Clear consciousness first establishes a basic *foothold* in the head's nerve-center above; but it reaches highest *awareness* by transforming the center farthest below. Between these two, the wondrous center of love reveals itself. This is the functional center of balance for true humanity and, therefore, true leadership. We depend on the heart center for our own peace and power, and we recognize it as the source of both freedom and love—toward which it will direct everyone we are called upon to serve.

We are reminded of Solomon's seal, in which an upward-turned triangle is interpenetrated by its downward-turned opposite. How does this ancient, prophetic symbol of the heart and its function shed light on the concept of leadership? It helps us to understand the picture of one who, as divine Lord and Master, achieves His hierarchically highest virtue by kneeling to wash the feet of the aspiring disciples and, ultimately, by choosing to sacrifice His very life for their forgiveness and renewal. Between the upward-striving effort of the disciples and the descending power of the divine light that seeks to uplift their world, there must be a rhythmic, heartfelt interaction. Foot-washing and then crucifixion bring heavenly grace into deep union with the earth.

Then, following its descent into the still darkness of the realm of departed souls who await deliverance, the divine act of love reverses itself. It becomes humanity's own nascent power to raise its consciousness and abilities to the keeper of truly creative love. "I, if I be lifted up," says the incarnating Christ spirit, "shall draw all of humankind unto me." This paradox associated with the heart realm, this enactment of Solomon's Seal, takes place in every act of genuine leadership.

Obedience

We return now to our original question: Should there be a real leader among teachers who wish to stand for true "responsibility and freedom?" Or should a group of capable teachers abhor the very idea and avoid the possibility of allowing a principal teacher to function with authority among them—a leader under whom they would, in a sense, have to consider themselves students? Emerson goes to the heart this matter:

> Who has more *obedience* than I masters me, though he should not raise his finger. Round him I must revolve by the gravitation of spirits.[3]

This is very different from "autocratic" power. We find this paradox of legitimate authority and power portrayed long ago in Scripture—for example, in Matthew 8:5–13 and in Luke 7:1–10:

> And a certain centurion's servant, who was dear to him, was sick, and ready to die. And when he heard of Jesus, he sent unto Him the elders of the Jews, beseeching Him to come and heal his servant.... Then Jesus went with them. And when He was now not far from the house, the centurion sent friends to Him, saying unto him, "Lord, trouble not yourself ... but say in a word, and my servant will be healed. For I also am a man set under authority, having under me soldiers, and I say unto one, Go, and he goes; and to another, Come, and he comes; and to my servant, Do this, and he does it."... And they that were sent, returning to the house, found the servant whole who had been sick.

The key word of special interest here is "under." Real authority has power only to the extent that it remains obediently

---

3. Emerson, "Self-Reliance."

under still higher authority. The Roman centurion is saying: My great power prevails just to the extent that I faithfully serve the Roman Empire; my power is therefore received by the grace of what is far higher than myself. And the centurion believed that Jesus, too, was in full charge only because He so dependably served the Father whom He knew to be higher than Himself. Only to the extent of His selfless obedience, therefore, did Jesus deserve, exercise, and transmit this higher power.

Nowadays—probably more than ever before—when teachers and leaders face problems in relation to their responsibilities, they should realize that they do not really know the essence of the answers required, and do not really have the power to do what must be done. Recognizing their actual ignorance and helplessness, they should rejoice in being able to seek counsel and strength from the world of light above. And they should do this with full confidence that their petitions will be heard and answered—so long as their sole motive is to know and do what is right. On this basis of shared trust, love, and the desire to be helpful, a practical working partnership can be established, which will in turn help to establish harmony and health on Earth. It is primarily through their own "obedient" example in this matter that genuine teachers and leaders (who do exist) can convey the fact of this opportunity and its necessity to those who have not closed their hearts against the very idea of leadership.

The authority of true leaders is justified because it functions humbly and under the freely recognized and chosen authority of a higher dimension. The nature of genuine humanity calls upon all of us to master ourselves before leading others. None of us can succeed in either of these efforts strictly on our own. We need—and should welcome—those, both in the heavenly world and here on Earth, who can supply the insight, love, and discipline we lack. The Roman centurion knew he had behind him the earthly power of Rome, and he recognized that Christ was backed by the power of the divine Father. Perhaps the centurion had heard some of the Savior's words:

> The Son can do nothing out of himself, but only what He sees the Father doing. Whatever the Father does, that the Son does, in His turn. (John 5:19)
>
> I can do nothing out of myself; I base my judgment on what I perceive in the realm of spirit, and my judgment is just; for I do not seek to satisfy my own will, but the will of Him who sent me. If I were only appearing as my own witness, my testimony would be without truth. (John 5:30–1)
>
> I have descended from heaven, not to do my will, but the will of Him who sent me. (John 6:38)

Genuine leadership should always be welcomed, for it represents grace released from above. Ultimately, we all identify with what is felt to be highest. This highest is not strange and foreign, since it is most deeply rooted in our own hearts. We come to feel truly at home through trusting fellowship, through a full-fledged identification with this wisdom, love, and power in the very center of our own being. Here is complete fulfillment and pure freedom.

"Are you not gods?" asked Christ. Creative godhood is both our source and that to which we aspire. The longing to *be* and to fulfill our potential waits within all of us, no matter how deeply buried in our lower self. Acquired materialism has dulled our inner consciousness, but for that very reason we should welcome the help of any other human being who is somewhat more steadily awake and aware than we are in certain essentials.

The purpose of spirit's descent—whether through leadership or in another form—is to serve us, and it makes possible our grateful ascent to serve in return.

Should we look up to such a leader among teachers as we would to a sure source of wisdom and virtue? Perhaps, but in our bewildering, hazardous time, no earthly knowledge or ability can adequately answer many of the questions confronting us. No mere human virtue can heal the sick, save the corrupt, harmonize the hateful, awaken love, and impart the confidence required by the dilemmas facing humanity today. Thus, we cannot expect paragons of wisdom and love for our guidance and encouragement. To some degree, all who live in the present time resemble the baffled disciples of Christ. They turned in helpless exasperation to the One they regarded as Lord and Master and asked the ultimate question: How can we possibly manage? His answer: "For that in us which is merely human, much is impossible that, for God in us, is possible. Everything is possible for God" (Mark 10:27). Teachers and leaders today must come to realize that what they impart to their students and followers will stand up to life's ultimate challenges only when it arises from conviction based on the personal experience that Christ's word is still right when it comes to understanding, compassion, and competence.

Attempts to probe the essential and to imagine the archetype of leadership may be valuable, but we must also mention actual practice—for example in an independent school, where originality and enterprise are necessary.

A school leader is sometimes allowed—and even asked—to designate a successor when leaving. More commonly, though, a majority vote of those to be served make that decision in a school community. The decision may be made by the board of trustees or the faculty, both of which are likely to share the same expectation—a new leadership that will fulfill two obligations: first, to heed their supervisory wishes, and second, to offer new direction. If the presumed school authorities, however, were to act in the spirit of leadership (as we have suggested) to be consistent with itself, it would reverse the order of these two obligations. The trustees, for example, might better understand that their own proper role is to support, in a flexible and positive way, the new leadership, and not just define the goals and methods. If they truly sense that they have a further leading role to play, they can prove it not through dominating but through service to the newly appointed leader.

One way to choose a candidate is to consider the majority vote decisive. A fairly large majority thus represents a "consensus," and what passes for consensus is considered the ideal. On the other hand, a quite different approach (much closer to the values emphasized in this discussion) will attract and do most to assure successful tenure for an authentic leader, or principal— one firmly committed to the policy of considering the greater practicality and consulting superior wisdom. Such a leader will rightly know that the present expectations and desires of those being served are not necessarily what they truly want in their hearts. They will be happier by joining their principal in setting aside mental habits and initial preferences and waiting, in emptiness and openness, for truths of a higher simpler quality. In this way, they can reach wholehearted agreement—quite unlike and far more effective than the "consensus" usually reached through negotiated compromise.[4]

---

4. Barry Morley does a remarkable job of clarifying the difference between "consensus" and a true "sense of the meeting," giving many examples to show how the latter is reached in group decisions in "Beyond Consensus, Salvaging the 'Sense of Meeting,'" Pendle Hill Publications, 1995.

Talk of "strong" leadership—especially praise—can raise questions about how a balance can be maintained. Do all members now become "followers," with the quality of leadership expected from only one? Don't all human beings occasionally seek and even find higher guidance without help from a central leader? This is a gift that can pass unpredictably around every circle. Does it not often happen that a quiet voice is raised unexpectedly and deserves to be heard despite its tentativeness? If encouraged, it can sometimes alter the whole sense of the meeting. Does this kind of event displace, or reinforce the value of a strong chairperson's leadership?

It should be clear that just the ability to discern and champion fresh truth when it speaks, however timidly, distinguishes the central leader among his or her colleagues. It is just this function that must be the real leader's specialty. The welcomed result for a faculty of teachers blessed by strong, central leadership will (perhaps surprisingly for some onlookers) be that every single member of this community—teachers, parents, and children—will be recognized and honored for leadership qualities (imagination, initiative, purpose, decisiveness, loyalty, and courage), each working in its proper sphere.[5]

The creative factor of being patient and trusting in "leadership from above," as discerned in the heart, is essential. Without this, and proceeding only with mental concepts of hard work, solidarity, and fair play, a group will probably lack the necessary discipline and power to initiate its goals with boldness and carry through at critical moments with decisiveness. There will be, rather, a tendency to engage in passionate and

5. In relation to this specific aspect, and to the whole question of leadership, see Heinz Zimmermann, *Speaking, Listening, Understanding: The Art of Creating Conscious Conversation*, Lindisfarne Press, Hudson, NY, 1996.

exhausting conflicts over convictions and stubbornly held preferences—and eliminating the objective and grateful sense of higher reason that make real solidarity possible.

Rather than disparaging and begrudging the idea of leadership, let us admire and welcome real leadership wherever it is given the chance to manifest. By trying to imagine its high possibilities and helping to realize them, we not only strengthen and balance it, but we come ever closer to the free creative authority through which we should be running our lives.

12.

THE DIRECT APPROACH
TO SPIRITUAL GUIDANCE

RUDOLF STEINER gave us the methods in the field of spiritual science, or anthroposophy, and some of their results. He inaugurated heart-warming, practical adventures in many areas of culture—for example, education, agriculture, medicine, science, art, social theory, and religion. He has shed real light on the reality and accessibility of Christ. Is there some way that we should be handling this treasure that we are neglecting?

After six decades as a student and worker in the field of anthroposophy, I have come to feel that what many fellow workers are so conscientiously trying to follow is at times not quite what they should be following. They may be trying to follow Steiner's teaching more than his example.

Steiner did not base his work on anyone's "teaching," neither traditional nor modern, religious nor scientific. He built empirically on direct spiritual experience—on knowledge that the living spirit is indeed both real and available. As a modern human soul, therefore, he felt both obliged and privileged to appeal directly to living spirit for the insight and strength he needed. The simple essence of the credo proclaimed by his example was this: I can ask, and I shall be answered—always in accord with the selflessness of my motive and with the real need for my request; this is true not because of my spiritual-scientific training, but because I am a human being who needs help and is trying to help others; what is true for me is no less true for every other seeker today, at whatever stage he or she may be.

Spiritual truth cannot be acquired second hand. Intellectual truths of the spirit are falsified when they become pride of knowledge. "Pride goes before destruction, and a haughty spirit before a fall" (Prov. 16:18). In the tenth of his lectures on St. John's Apocalypse, Rudolf Steiner interrupted one of his own complex accounts of humanity's spiritual development through the ages, to insert this consoling but cautionary observation:

> As long as you build up a scaffolding, you remain in the thought realm you are accustomed to in the physical world. The whole scheme we have sketched here is only physical thought. It is related to the complete structure, but in a way similar to the outer scaffolding upon which the builders stand. This has to be taken down when the building is completed. In the same way, *the scaffolding of thought has to be taken down if one wishes to have the truth before one as it really is....* Therefore one must take care not to confuse real occult wisdom with what is struggled for using physical means of comprehension, which wants to standardize the higher worlds. (emphasis added)[1]

We often succumb to the kind of physical thinking about spiritual "information" that, although it does its best to remain true to gifts received from the past, inevitably tends to fail the

---

1. *The Apocalypse of St. John*, Rudolf Steiner Press, London, 1985, pp. 180–181.

test of present reality. In other words: Will we accomplish the greatest good for humanity and our Earth through the "lore" of spiritual science (valid and necessary, though it is), or is there a more fundamental orientation from which spiritual science itself originated and which that science now depends on for its appropriate evolution?

Rudolf Steiner repeatedly pointed to the crisis that would become more and more threatening toward the end of the twentieth century and the beginning of the third millennium. He considered the unprecedented abundance of spiritual wisdom that he, among others, was graced to receive and transmit to be a specific, indispensable preparation for this time. In the earthly battle of Michael with the mighty Dragon and "prince of this world," Steiner envisioned a decisive role for the spiritual teachings and cultural initiatives he was destined to deliver. But in order for these to become the pillars of strength humanity will need for future trials, he never failed to emphasize that spirit knowledge must become in us not only mental conviction but a creative, life-transforming force of heart and will. The way will open for higher worlds to work among us when spirit knowledge becomes the source of the love that conquers fear.

To lift mere intellectual insights to inspired creative Truth requires love. Love rises most humbly (yet abundantly) from hearts that have come to realize that they do not really know what they think they know; the power that seems to be given with mere conceptual knowledge of the spirit is not yet vital power. Such hearts have learned that, for truly creative power, they must turn to higher sources—primarily, and ever renewed, to the divine human Being who through His love came to help us in all things.

The right relationship between what we read and hold in our minds as conceptual knowledge "about" the spirit, and the creative, transforming love of the Redeemer—whose living wisdom awaits each day and moment to be consulted by every human heart—is characterized by Saint Paul in a familiar way. Today it carries a special message for students of Steiner:

> If I speak out of the Spirit with the tongues of human beings and angels; if I am without love, then my speaking remains as sounding brass or tinkling cymbal. And if I had the gift of prophecy and could speak of all mysteries and could impart all knowledge and, further, had the power of faith that removes mountains; if I am without love, then I am nothing. And if I were to give away everything that is mine ... if I am without love, then all is in vain.

> If love is truly present it cannot be lost. The gift of prophecy must one day be extinguished, the wonder of languages cease, clairvoyant insight come to an end. Our insight is incomplete, incomplete is our prophecy. But one day the perfect must come, the complete consecration-aim; then the time of the incomplete is over. (1 Cor. 13:1–3, 8–10)

Few of us aspire at all to become "scientists" of the spirit. We are simply trying to get on with our lives under guidance in basic matters and trying to help others do the same. In the context of our own small responsibilities, what we crave is simply a modest kind of understanding as a form of *love*, to give us strength to survive and serve. That is all. For this purpose, we urgently need daily divine companionship, counsel, and encouragement.

If, indeed, we must wait until we have graduated, as it were, from a training for spiritual scientists before having the right to ask for and receive answers from heaven, for most of us the prospects are certainly bleak. For, if without this "diploma" we nevertheless do ask, we can hardly expect that the questions we lift from below will receive trustworthy answers—or indeed, any—from above.

But perhaps the fearful part of our souls is sometimes secretly grateful for the distance that seems to separate us amateurs from spirit reality. Perhaps most of our questions simply want practical problems relieved and personal protection, and perhaps the soul prefers to be shielded from direct contact with the spirit it addresses. "Dear God," this perhaps unconscious self may be saying, "please remove my painful concern. I know you won't really tell me about it (and I won't ask you to explain), just do it. Whenever I think of what I imagine as your uncompromising righteousness, I confess that I fear coming too close to you. I am ignorant and unworthy, and I admit that my comfort, for now, depends on my remaining so. The sign on my door indicates that my fear exceeds even my shame: 'Please! Do not disturb!'"

The response might be: "Your faith in me whom you cannot see is noble and deserving, but your fear is unwarranted. I want you to know that as directly and trustingly as you ask my help, so will I *always* respond—regardless of mistakes you will certainly make at times—both in the accuracy of your hearing and in the soundness of your interpretation. Trust my love to make good on such mistakes, without blame. I have and always will come to help. Let us be friends."

When truth is sought, the loving power of Truth itself must be fully believed in. Whereas we may imagine that conscientious hesitancy and scrupulous doubting are essential in the search for truth, these will never open the door to higher experience. Doubting one's *own* ability to draw upon spiritual truth is justified; but doubting the *spirit's* ability to compensate for one's personal inadequacy in honest asking and listening arises from a counterforce—one that will always find further excuses for fear of the requirements and responsibilities of direct contact with divine spirit. When we heed this counterforce, most of our own deserved self-doubt gets undeservedly transferred and becomes an inability to trust the higher Being to whom we think we are humbly appealing.

New faculties of the soul have long been ripening, and the time has come when they can allow humanity to be intimately and genuinely aware of Christ's knowing, healing presence. But how can we approach Christ directly with questions about our earthly problems? Rudolf Steiner indicated the way:

> Christ is not merely a ruler of human beings, but their brother. The time must come and cannot be far distant when human souls will, in their immortal part, learn to ask of Christ whenever they think of undertaking something: Should we do this, or not? Then human souls will find Christ standing beside them as the beloved Companion; and they will obtain not only consolation and strength from the Christ Being, but will receive also instruction from Him as to what is to be done.... *Humanity, however, must learn to ask of Him.* (Emphasis added)[2]

---

2. Rudolf Steiner, *Cosmic and Human Metamorphoses,* lecture 1, Anthroposophical Publishing Co., London, 1926.

In most cases this asking does not issue from spiritually trained minds, but from the simplicity and earnestness of contrite hearts—not from knowledge, but from the loving trust that moves toward enlightenment. This approach may correctly consider itself unworthy, but it speaks an eloquent language swiftly heard and always met by the Redeemer. His response issues from the context of higher wisdom, but his acceptance comes through answers expressed in the ways most accessible to those who have asked.

The task of spiritual science today is to make it possible for hitherto skeptical minds to perceive once again the central role of unwavering faith in the quest for a direct relationship to living spirit. The faith now possible is not the same as that which followed the decline of spiritual vision in times past. Although earlier faith came to be recognized as "blind," the new faith, in contrast, effectively works to open closed eyes. It lifts the veil to reveal clear awareness.

Let us call such guidance the "direct approach" to spiritual awareness. The appeal here comes from the reverent and courageous heart, whose intuitive quest must precede any formulation in spiritual-scientific terms. This path will no doubt include enthusiastic study of wisdom teachings as directed by destiny, but, primarily, we do not depend on these teachings in the conduct of our lives. Such profound and comprehensive truths are fortunately available for our instruction and encouragement, but the most direct path still awaits.

It may occur to young seekers that they really have no right to hope for direct dialogue with the world of light and love. But this intimate contact is a life-necessity and, therefore, a privilege granted to all. Trustworthy guidance must come to the naive as well as to the experienced. But how can beginners relate their small inspirations to the powerful, extensive wisdom communicated by a high master such as Rudolf Steiner?

The master's wisdom is far broader and deeper than most, but, whereas it is "mature," it may be perceived as "old," since we receive it in printed form as a legacy from the past. As ripened fruit, maturity contains an inexhaustible multitude of seeds for the present and future, but these are capable of bringing forth new life only when drawn from the fruit. True wisdom always takes care to step back a pace. It must fall, so to speak, and even fall apart, so that its seeds may come forth. Its own cherished goal, henceforth, is less to be remembered and consulted than to be altogether and thoroughly reborn—both from the ground upward and from the heights downward.

The fruit of wisdom as such is never of primary importance, but rather the fruiting process itself, which must continue intact. Whereas wisdom appears, in a sense, to utter the "final word," youth's guidance must be recognized for the timeliness of its "first words." Thus, the evolution of spiritual truth is vital and fruitful only when both age and youth realize that they have something indispensable to give each other. Such truth will always be fresh and changing.

Age, as the teacher, sets the example and should be loved for it; whereas it slows youth by insisting on keen discernment, it thus also facilitates and hastens sound progress. Age has sifted life-experience for its meaning, and youth now calls *new* experience into being. Youth is urged primarily to *be* and to *do*— with the confidence that new deeds will render old knowledge truly useful. From actions that are timely, valiant, and loving (if not always "wise"), experience will surely find new ways to *become* wisdom.

The New Country

Can you bring your whole being to the frontier daily?
The frontier is inward now, not outward.
It is waiting to be explored.

The spirit is often obscured by talk of the spirit.
All the books, gadgets, odds and ends, and superstitions
people attach to themselves in the name of spirit —
one must be able to hack through that jungle.
The best weapon is the direct approach.
In fact, now it is the only weapon.

Each soul looking directly to Me.
Each soul being ready and willing to leave all comfort
behind,
Each soul being ready to listen for and stand up for Me,
regardless of what may happen to friends, family, financial
security,
As this is done, the new country will come into view.[3]

---

3. *Turning*, "The New Country," p.51.

Further Reading

Anonymous. *Turning*, Anthroposophic Press, Hudson, NY, 1994.

Bock, Emil. *The Apocalypse of St. John*, Floris Books, Edinburgh, 1986.

Brooks, Van Wyck. *The Life of Emerson*, E. P. Dutton & Co., New York, 1932.

Bucke, Richard M. *Cosmic Consciousness,* Dutton & Co., New York, 1923.

Byrd, Admiral Richard E. *Alone*, G.P. Putnam's Sons, New York, 1938.

Carlyle, Thomas. *On Heroes, Hero-Worship, and the Heroic in History*, Oxford University Press, London.

Childs, Gilbert. *Rudolf Steiner: His Life and Work*, Anthroposophic Press, Hudson, NY, 1995.

Dewey, John. *Experience and Nature*, The Open Court Publishing Company, LaSalle, Illinois, 1929.

Dunselman, Ron. *In Place of the Self: How Drugs Work*, Hawthorn Press, Stroud, U.K., 1995.

Elium, Don and Jeanne. *Raising a Son*, Beyond Words Publishing Inc., Hillsboro, OR, 1992.

—— *Raising a Daughter*, Celestial Arts, Berkeley, CA, 1994.

—— *Raising a Family*, Celestial Arts, Berkeley, CA, 1997.

Emerson, Ralph Waldo. *Essays and Poems*, Selected and introduced by Tony Tanner, Everyman's Library, Charles E. Tuttle Co., Inc., Rutland, Vermont, 1992.

—— *The Selected Writings of Ralph Waldo Emerson*, The Modern Library, Random House, Inc., NY, 1950.

—— *The Complete Writings of Ralph Waldo Emerson,* Wm. H. Wise & Co., NY, 1929.

Frankl, Viktor. *Man's Search for Meaning,* Touchstone Books, New York, 1984.

Gardner, John Fentress. *Education in Search of the Spirit: Essays on American Education,* Anthroposophic Press, Hudson, NY, 1996.

—— *American Heralds of the Spirit: Emerson, Whitman, and Melville,* Anthroposophic Press, Hudson, NY, 1992.

Juenger, Friedrich Georg. *The Failure of Technology,* Henry Regnery Company, Chicago, 1949.

Koepke, Hermann. *On the Threshold of Adolescence: The Struggle for Independence in the Twelfth Year,* Anthroposophic Press, NY, 1992.

Rittelmeyer, Friedrich. *Rudolf Steiner Enters My Life,* Floris Books, Edinburgh, 1982.

Schumacher, E. F. *Small is Beautiful,* Harper & Row, New York, 1973.

Shepherd, A. P. *A Scientist of the Invisible,* Inner Traditions, Rochester, VT, 1987.

Staley, Betty. *Between Form and Freedom,* Hawthorn Press, Stroud, U.K., 1988.

Steiner, Rudolf. *The Child's Changing Consciousness and Waldorf Education,* Anthroposophic Press, Hudson, NY, 1996.

—— *Cosmic and Human Metamorphoses,* lecture 1, Anthroposophical Publishing Co., London, 1926.

—— *The Course of My Life,* Anthroposophic Press, Hudson, NY, 1986.

—— *The Education of the Child, And Early Lectures on Education.* Anthroposophic Press, Hudson, NY, 1996.

—— *Education for Adolescents,* Anthroposophic Press, Hudson, NY, 1996.

—— *The Genius of Language: Observations for Teachers,* Hudson, NY, Anthroposophic Press, 1995.

—— *Goethean Science*, Mercury Press, Spring Valley, NY, 1988.

—— *How to Know Higher Worlds: A Modern Path of Initiation*, Anthroposophic Press, Hudson, NY, 1994.

—— *Intuitive Thinking as a Spiritual Path: A Philosophy of Freedom*, Anthroposophic Press, Hudson, NY, 1995.

—— *The Kingdom of Childhood: Introductory Talks on Waldorf Education*, Anthroposophic Press, Hudson, NY, 1995.

—— *The Spirit of the Waldorf School: Lectures Surrounding the Founding of the First Waldorf School, Stuttgart*–1919, Hudson, Anthroposophic Press, NY, 1995.

—— *Stages of Higher Knowledge*, Anthroposophic Press, Spring Valley, NY, 1967.

—— *A Theory of Knowledge*, Anthroposophic Press, Spring Valley, NY, 1968.

—— *The Threefold Social Order*, Anthroposophic Press, Spring Valley, NY, 1966.

—— *Waldorf Education and Anthroposophy 1: Public Lectures 1921–22*, Anthroposophic Press, Hudson, NY, 1995.

—— *Waldorf Education and Anthroposophy 2: Public Lectures 1923–24*, Anthroposophic Press, Hudson, NY, 1996.

Talbott, Stephen L. *The Future Does Not Compute: Transcending the Machines in Our Midst*, O'Reilly and Associates, Inc., Stabastapol, CA, 1995.

Treichler, Rudolf. *Soulways: Development, crises and illnesses of the soul*, Hawthorn Press, Stroud, U.K., 1996.

Winkler, Franz E. *Man: The Bridge between Two Worlds*, Waldorf Press, Garden City, NY, 1975.

—— *For Freedom Destined*, Waldorf Press, Garden City, NY, 1974.

Zimmermann, Heinz. *Speaking, Listening, Understanding: The Art of Creating Conscious Conversation*, Lindisfarne Press, Hudson, NY, 1996.

. . . .

*For an informative catalog of the work of Rudolf Steiner
and other anthroposophical authors please contact*

ANTHROPOSOPHIC PRESS
RR 4 Box 94 A-1 Hudson, NY 12534
TEL: 518 851 2054
FAX: 518 851 2047